Chicken Soup
for the Soul.

Think
Positive
for Preteens

Chicken Soup for the Soul: Think Positive for Preteens
Amy Newmark

Published by Chicken Soup for the Soul, LLC www.chickensoup.com
Copyright ©2020 by Chicken Soup for the Soul, LLC. All Rights Reserved.

The publisher gratefully acknowledges the many publishers and individuals who granted Chicken Soup for the Soul permission to reprint the cited material.

Front and back cover images: Torn paper collage courtesy of iStockphoto.com/trinetuzun (©trinetuzun), head phones courtesy of iStockphoto.com/mecaleha (©mecaleha), Sneaker courtesy of iStockphoto.com/sntpzh (©sntpzh), ice pop courtesy of iStockphoto.com/Kuzmik_A (©Kuzmik_A), illustration of Pegasus horse courtesy of iStockphoto.com/Tomacco (©Tomacco), illustration of heart courtesy of iStockphoto.com/blue67 (©blue67), illustration of girl jumping courtesy of iStockphoto.com/nuranvectorgirl (©nuranvectorgirl), photo of kids courtesy of iStockphoto.com/monkeybusinessimages (©monkeybusinessimages)

Interior pages: photo frames courtesy of iStockphoto.com/GoodGnom (©GoodGnom), star and flower drawings courtesy of iStockphoto.com/blue67 (©blue67), page 5 photo courtesy of iStockphoto.com/twinsterphoto (©twinsterphoto), page 11 illustration courtesy of iStockphoto.com/dorian2013 (©dorian2013), page 34 photo courtesy of iStockphoto.com/monkeybusinessimages (©monkeybusinessimages), page 39 illustration courtesy of iStockphoto.com/dorian2013 (©dorian2013), page 61 photo courtesy of iStockphoto.com/PeopleImages (©PeopleImages), page 67 photo courtesy of iStockphoto.com/Deagreez (©Deagreez), page 87 illustration courtesy of iStockphoto.com/elfiny (©elfiny), page 95 photo courtesy of iStockphoto.com/monkeybusinessimages (©monkeybusinessimages), page 121 photo courtesy of iStockphoto.com/FatCamera (©Aiden-Franklin), page 141 illustration courtesy of iStockphoto.com/Kaewta Sirimongkolwattana (©Kaewta Sirimongkolwattana), page 146 photo courtesy of iStockphoto.com/MaFelipe (©MaFelipe), page 169 illustration courtesy of iStockphoto.com/aleksandarvelasevic (©aleksandarvelasevic), page 177 photo courtesy of iStockphoto.com/AzmanL (©AzmanL), page 201 illustration courtesy of iStockphoto.com/Andrei Filippov (©Andrei Filippov), page 207 photo courtesy of iStockphoto.com/Poike (©Poike), page 219 illustration courtesy of iStockphoto.com/natasha-tpr (©natasha-tpr), page 225 hand illustration courtesy of iStockphoto.com/NatBasil (©NatBasil), sun illustration courtesy of iStockphoto.com/ulimi (©ulimi)
Photo of Amy Newmark courtesy of Susan Morrow at SwickPix

Cover and Interior by Daniel Zaccari

Distributed to the booktrade by Simon & Schuster. SAN: 200-2442

Publisher's Cataloging-In-Publication Data
(Prepared by The Donohue Group, Inc.)

Names: Newmark, Amy, compiler.
Title: Chicken soup for the soul : think positive for preteens / [compiled by] Amy Newmark.
Other Titles: Think positive for preteens
Description: [Cos Cob, Connecticut] : Chicken Soup for the Soul, LLC, [2020] | Interest age level: 008-012. | "A compilation of personal, revealing stories about preteens' real-life experiences that provides a roadmap for preteens to be the very best they can be. Values such as friendship, gratitude, honesty, self-respect, family bonding, open-mindedness, persistence, and trying new things are illustrated by the stories. Some stories are followed by quizzes or inspirational quotes that reinforce the lessons learned in the stories"—Provided by publisher.
Identifiers: ISBN 9781611599954 | ISBN 9781611592955 (ebook)
Subjects: LCSH: Preteens--Conduct of life--Literary collections--Juvenile literature. | Preteens--Conduct of life--Anecdotes--Juvenile literature. | Self-esteem--Literary collections--Juvenile literature. | Self-esteem--Anecdotes--Juvenile literature. | CYAC: Conduct of life--Literary collections. | Conduct of life--Anecdotes. | Self-esteem--Literary collections. | Self-esteem--Anecdotes. | LCGFT: Anecdotes.
Classification: LCC BJ1631 .C453 2020 (print) | LCC BJ1631 (ebook) | DDC 158.10834--dc23

PRINTED IN THE UNITED STATES OF AMERICA
on acid∞free paper

25 24 23 22 21 20   01 02 03 04 05 06 07 08 09 10 11

Chicken Soup for the Soul

for the Soul.

Think Positive for Preteens

Amy Newmark

CSS

Chicken Soup for the Soul, LLC
Cos Cob, CT

Changing the world one story at a time®
www.chickensoup.com

CONTENTS

❶
JUST BE YOU

❷
MAKE TRUE FRIENDS

❸
DO THE RIGHT THING

❹
GO AHEAD AND TRY IT

❺
FACE YOUR CHALLENGES

❻
COUNT YOUR BLESSINGS

❼
TREASURE YOUR FAMILY

8
LOOK PAST THE OBVIOUS

INTRODUCTION

Welcome to a new kind of *Chicken Soup for the Soul* book for preteens. The stories in this book will help you "think positive." They will help you be the very best, happiest version of yourself.

We know that being a kid can be tough. Your bodies are changing, your schoolwork is getting harder, and your parents are giving you more responsibility. Your friends are changing too. Sometimes you end up joining a new group of friends. Sometimes you switch best friends. You're figuring out who you are and who you want to become; that means making new friends, trying new activities, and even changing your look!

Chapter 1 is called "Just Be You." You'll meet some kids who had to figure out who they were, just like you. Sometimes that meant starting a new lunch table, with the less "popular" but way more fun kids. Sometimes that meant getting over embarrassment for something that made them different, like stuttering or being the biggest kid in the class.

Have you ever said you needed new friends? Chapter 2 is called "Make True Friends." You'll read stories from preteens who realized that they didn't want to be friends with kids who didn't respect them. They found new, true friends. They also learned some lessons about loyalty when they stood up for those friends against bullies.

Standing up for what you believe is important. Chapter 3 is called "Do the Right Thing." You'll meet a girl who said the Pledge of Allegiance even when other kids made fun of her. You'll meet kids who told the truth about something they had done, and how much better they felt afterward. And you'll meet kids who surprised themselves by volunteering to do something nice — they learned how good it made them feel.

You're at the age when you have the opportunity to try lots of new things. Some of those new things might even be a little scary. They might be things like helping an elderly neighbor, or appearing in a play, or starting a new sport. Chapter 4 is called "Go Ahead and Try It." You'll read stories by kids who took the risk and tried new things, and were so happy they did.

There are so many challenges that kids face — starting at a new school, having a disease, or looking different from everyone else are just a few of them. Chapter 5 is called "Face Your Challenges." You'll meet kids who share their stories about how they managed to stay happy and confident while handling their problems.

No matter what's going on in your life, it's important to be grateful for what you have. This is what adults do to help them through all the ups and downs of life. That's why we included Chapter 6, which is called "Count Your Blessings." You'll meet kids who realized what was really important. They stopped asking for the latest fashions or technology. Instead, they focused on all the good things in their lives.

Being grateful for your parents and siblings and grandparents matters, too, even if you sometimes take them for granted. Chapter 7 is called "Treasure Your Family." You'll meet all kinds of kids with all kinds of families. They share their personal stories about how special their family members really are.

Chapter 8 is where we surprise you. It's called "Look Past the Obvious." You'll read about popular kids who are secretly very insecure. You'll also read some great ideas for how to stop a bully. It turns out that treating a bully like a friend is sometimes enough to fix the problem.

As you journey through these pages, you'll also find some fun quizzes, quotes, and coloring pages hidden among the stories. We hope you will have fun with this new kind of *Chicken Soup for the Soul* book, designed just for you.

— Amy Newmark —
Editor-in-Chief and Publisher
Chicken Soup for the Soul

Chapter
1

JUST BE YOU

The Real Popular Table

*A friend can tell you things you don't want
to tell yourself.*
-Frances Ward Weller

All I wanted was to sit with them. Jill had the best clothes. She looked like she walked straight out of a store window. Julie wore blush and lip gloss. Brett had the coolest haircut, plus she was already on the varsity field hockey team and we were only in the sixth grade! Crystal had a boyfriend, Aimee was a cheerleader and Shannon could boss people around and they'd do whatever she said. I sure didn't have that kind of power, but then again, I wasn't popular.

Everyone else called them the "popular girls" and at lunch I'd watch them from across the middle school cafeteria and wonder how on earth I could get a seat at their table. I imagined how much fun they had sitting there, the envy of the lunchroom, while I picked at my soggy PB&J at the table near the trash cans. This wasn't how I thought middle school was going to be at all. One day, I'd had the nerve to walk past their table and Shannon and Jill had started making fun of me, saying I smelled. Shannon called me a "scum." That was what the popular girls laughingly called all of the non-popular girls. They thought it was hilarious and it was even funnier when Julie pointed out that she'd seen my sneakers on the clearance rack at Dollar General. It was true though. My family couldn't afford shoes like the popular girls wore.

I had three friends. We knew each other from elementary school and rode the same bus, which was, of course, not the same bus as the popular girls because they all lived in the new, fancy subdivision outside of town. My friends were "scums" too. One of them was super smart, another super shy and the third was just super weird, but she could always make us laugh. They were the ones I sat with at lunch.

"I hate them," I sighed, slumping down into my seat beside my three friends and opening my lunch bag. "The popular girls are so mean."

"Well, we aren't mean!" said my weird friend, and she was right.

I looked towards the popular table. Aimee appeared to be in a fight with Jill, while the other four had ganged up on a nerdy, red-headed boy, who was easily the smartest kid in our grade and maybe even our whole school. He was practically in tears when they got done with him. He took his tray to an empty table in the far corner of the room to eat alone.

That was when it hit me. Why would I even want to be

friends with people who were so mean? My friends were far nicer and from the looks of it, we had a lot more fun. None of us fought or made fun of people. We laughed, sang, joked, traded stickers and spent our lunch hour making up hilarious skits to act out and entertain one another.

> **Why would I even want to be friends with people who were so mean?**

"Hey," I said gesturing towards the lonely, red-haired boy, "Maybe I should ask him to come eat with us."

"Sure," said my friends.

He sat with us every day after that, which was great because he helped me with my science homework.

From then on, we made a point to invite everyone the popular girls made fun of to eat at our lunch table. Soon our table was filled and we had to add more chairs, all of us willing to scoot in just a little closer to make room for someone else. It may have been a little cramped, but at our table, everyone fit regardless of whether or not they were fat, dressed funny, came from a poor family, didn't shop at the trendy stores, played tuba in band, were obsessed with *Dungeons and Dragons*, or were funny looking. I started to look forward to lunchtime. Middle school was turning out to be a lot of fun after all.

Around Christmas, the popular girls banished Aimee from their group. We never asked why and it didn't matter when she came to our table and meekly asked to sit down. Of course we let her in and she looked relieved. I offered her an Oreo from my lunch bag and she thanked me.

"Wow, it's so nice to be away from them. I used to look at you guys over here and wish I could have as much fun as you," Aimee said.

"No way," I replied in disbelief. "I used to wish I could sit at your table!"

I looked around and realized how silly I had been. Almost twenty kids now sat happily at what was once the "scum" table. We were laughing, sharing, smiling. I glanced back at the popular girls with their perfect outfits and hair. There were only five of them now. They rolled their eyes and wrinkled their noses, pushed their food away. They teased a short girl and mocked a boy who was in Special Ed classes and the whole time they looked completely miserable.

> We made a point to invite everyone the popular girls made fun of to eat at our lunch table.

Later, I looked up the word "popular" in the dictionary. It meant to be liked by a lot of people. Hardly anyone liked the popular girls at school. They didn't even seem to like each other or themselves very much. When I looked at my group of friends, which seemed to grow every day, I understood where the true "popular table" was in our middle school cafeteria and knew that I had gotten my wish after all.

— Victoria Fedden —
Chicken Soup for the Soul: Think Positive for Kids

Popular

pop·u·lar

adjective

liked, admired, or enjoyed by many people

My Own Label

*If you doubt yourself, then indeed you
stand on shaky ground.*
—Henrik Ibsen

It seemed to me that I had two different identities when I was in fifth grade. Outside of school, I was a reasonably happy kid who enjoyed spending time with her friends, reading about ancient Egypt, and listening to rock music. When I was in class, however, I turned into a very different Denise, one who was on guard all the time — one who wanted nothing more than to get through the day without being teased.

To my classmates I was weird, because I wasn't just like them. They focused on that which was most obvious — that I didn't wear the same name brand designer clothes that they did. In my class, where everyone worked overtime at being fashionable, this was no light offense. The class photo was a parade of designer labels — expensive shoes and sweaters with conspicuous logos, shirts with embroidered marks, and jeans with glittery patches and buttons. Even their hair accessories had little designer tags.

Designer clothes were beyond my family's reach. My mother was a single parent, and she worked long hours to support our small household. In the currencies of love and attention, I was rich beyond all imagination. I was adored, supported and cared for. The only currency my classmates dealt in was fashion, though, and there, I was poor. There just wasn't any justification for spending the entire clothing budget on one silly shirt or pair of jeans that happened to have a label the cool kids liked.

In the currencies of love and attention, I was rich beyond all imagination.

I never knew if my classmates would torment me in class, but on the bus I could count on it. My trips to and from school were the horrific, painful bookends to stressful days. Sometimes my classmates insulted me to my face; at other times, I merely heard the snickers behind me. One girl made a point of running down the aisle every morning to see what I was wearing, and then returned to her friends to laugh about it. I shrank into myself and stared out the window.

I was the smallest girl in my class. One of my classmates' mothers noticed, and offered me a denim skirt that her daughter had outgrown. I wore it happily, thrilled to have a cool item of clothing for once. When I outgrew the skirt, my mother bought me a new one of my own, albeit one without a label. When my classmate saw it, she hooted. "Oh, that's not my skirt, is it? Where did you get this one, Denise?" she sneered. "The poorhouse?" My classmates giggled, and I slunk away, my eyes locked on the ground. I stopped wearing the skirt.

After fifth grade ended, over the summer, I spent a month at day camp, where I found kids who liked me for who I was, not for the clothes I wore. Many of them came from wealthy families, and I spotted plenty of designer shoes, high fashion swimsuits and T-shirts that cost three figures. Unlike the kids at school, though, my fellow campers didn't mind my no-name wardrobe. They simply accepted me as a friend. We spent our days splashing around in the pool, riding horses, and making bracelets. We had a fashion show and I was encouraged to participate. And I did. My weekends were filled with fun with my best friend in the neighborhood, who would have liked me even if I'd shown up at her house in a potato sack dress.

With the love and support of my friends, I started to remember something I'd forgotten: there was nothing wrong with me. Nothing at all. It wasn't my fault that my classmates had targeted me. They were only one small, cruel group of people, and there was no reason to pay any attention to them at all.

It took a while for the message to sink in, though. When sixth grade started, my classmates resumed their bullying. For the first few months of school, I was desperately unhappy. The warm glow of friendship I had fostered over the summer was dimmed by the open hostility and insults I faced every day in class.

Finally, I begged my mother for a fashion shirt. I liked the garment for its design, but more than that, I thought that it would be an antidote for the bullying. I knew that my classmates were so shallow that they only looked at my wardrobe. I didn't want to impress them or be friends with them. If I dressed just like them, though, maybe they'd run out of reasons to bother me.

The shirt did not appear for my eleventh birthday in November. Wishes do come true, though, even if they take time, and somehow, on Christmas morning, there was a very special green and white box waiting under the tree for me.

I'd finally met their approval... and yet, I knew that I didn't even want it.

When I went back to school after the holiday recess, I proudly wore my new shirt. For once, nobody mocked me when I boarded the bus. Instead, they stared. The girls in my class were so upset that they actually held a meeting in the library to talk about it. I tried not to laugh as I saw them clustered around a table, whispering and looking furtively in my direction. One of them ran up to me, grabbed me by the shoulder, and yanked at my collar to look at the tag. Her breath caught, and I realized that she hadn't expected the shirt to be authentic.

On the bus that afternoon, one of my classmates told me that she liked my outfit. I smiled and nodded. I'd finally met their approval... and yet, I knew that I didn't even want it. What they thought, or didn't think, about me was irrelevant. I was the exact same person they had tormented before the holidays.

Moreover, I wasn't wearing my shirt to impress them; I was wearing it because I liked it. The only label that mattered to me was my own — how I "labeled" myself. It was something they would never comprehend.

> The one person I had to learn to impress was myself, and I'd done it.

After that day, my classmates still bothered me, but I stopped listening. Their taunts weren't worth even a moment of my time. Instead of getting upset, I was bored by their remarks.

In the spring, the denim skirt that my classmate had mocked made a reappearance. I wore it proudly to both the school dance festival and to my sixth-grade graduation ceremony.

There would be no diploma for positive thinking, no award for finally learning to ignore cruel words. There never would be. The one person I had to learn to impress was myself, and I'd done it.

— Denise Reich —
Chicken Soup for the Soul: Just for Preteens

List 3 things that shouldn't matter (like size or clothing)

1.

2.

3.

List 3 things that should matter (like how you treat people)

1.

2.

3.

More Than Good Enough

He who trims himself to suit everyone will soon whittle himself away.
~Raymond Hull

It seems like the second you step into middle school, you get judged. Not by other people, but instead by yourself. It's like a constant buzzing going on in your head—an endless circle of thoughts composed of questions for yourself like, "How does my hair look?" or maybe, "Would answering this history question make me look like a snob?" and the always persistent, "Am I good enough?"

> It seems like the second you step into middle school, you get judged.

I made the bulk of my friends during the first month of school. I always talked to a wide group of personalities, so I knew people who listened to music that screamed at you, people who wore heels bigger than their feet, people who listened to hip hop (which I am much more inclined to listen to, although I never told anyone), and ones who looked like they walked straight out of one of those teen novels, fully equipped with tubes of lip gloss and pink purses.

Then I knew a boy — his name was Brian. He almost always had his earphones placed firmly in his ears (but heard and responded to everything I said), wore what he called "vintage shoes," and was an active member of the Boy Scouts. He was the guy who was different from everyone else. I thought people's stares would faze him, but they didn't. In fact, Brian welcomed negative comments and simply questioned others about the way they lead their own lives. Something about him always made me feel nervous but oddly at ease: Brian never judged me or said anything about the way I looked or what I said. Looking back, it made me nervous because I wasn't used to it.

When I wasn't with Brian, I was constantly trying to be like the people I would speak to. My grades started to slip, the loud music I listened to started to give me headaches, and I was spending the little money I had on clothes and shoes. In short, my life was a complete mess. It was clear I had caved into the pressure of middle school. It was like I was in a hole and I just kept digging.

One day, somewhere in the middle of the third month of school, I was sitting behind Brian in Algebra class. I had just gotten back a polynomial test with a big red sixty-eight percent scrawled across the top. That test was the worst grade I had gotten in at least five years. I was usually such a good student — I did not understand what was happening to my grades.

Before I had the chance to shove the paper in my bag so no one would see it, Brian turned around with a neutral expression, a one hundred percent test in his hand.

"That's because you focus too much attention on what other people think about you," he said to me, gesturing towards my not-so-stellar test. "For someone so smart, you act like such an idiot when it comes to other people." I wasn't even sure how to respond.

"What's that supposed to mean?" I asked.

"It means that you never act like yourself. I always see you change the song you're listening to when certain people walk by. And you never answer questions in class that I'm sure you know."

"That's not true," I lied.

"Yes, it is. Just stop caring about what people think. Don't try to change yourself; you're just fine the way you are when you talk to me," he said before turning around to face the blackboard.

"You never act like yourself."

I could feel my mouth hanging wide open, but I couldn't concentrate long enough to close it. Had Brian just told me that I shouldn't try to fit in? I thought this was middle school, where people had to make friends if they wanted to make it through high school. Yet there Brian was, sitting comfortably in his own little world, with perfect grades and a collected life. And then there was me — breaking down on the inside, horrible grades, and a generally miserable life. I must have been missing something.

I realized that Brian was right. It was time for me to listen to the music I wanted to listen to, dress the way I wanted to dress, and to take control of my middle school life regardless of what my other classmates thought of me. I realized that if you're not happy with yourself, you can't have a happy middle school experience. So I took Brian's advice and started to act like myself, and I noticed that I was more than good enough. Finally.

— Jackson Beard —
Chicken Soup for the Soul: Teens Talk Middle School

Holy Calves

When you're always trying to conform to the
norm, you lose your uniqueness, which can be
the foundation for your greatness.
~Dale Archer

My father was the first one to point out my unusually large leg muscles. I was just a gangly kid, maybe ten or eleven, and I'd never thought about the shape of my body before.

"You've got legs just like your mother," he said with a smile, ruffling my blond hair.

After he made that comment, I started scrutinizing other girls' legs and comparing them to my own. I could tell that my legs were different, and when you're a kid, being different is not a good thing.

I stood in front of the mirror and inspected my legs from every angle. From the front, my calf muscles jutted out so much that they joined together in the middle. From the side, they bulged out like baseball bats, hard and bulbous. From the back, they were inconceivably large. If I stood on my tippy toes, my calf muscles appeared thinner from the front, but even bigger from the back and side.

My leg muscles were enormous no matter which way I turned. Why couldn't I just have stick-straight legs like the other girls in my class?

To top it all off, my mother wouldn't let me shave them. To put it simply, I had man legs. What had I ever done to deserve such muscular legs? I had the body of a pro athlete, but besides a few stints of soccer and swimming, I wasn't all that athletic.

Middle school gym class was the worst part of my week. Sitting beside the cool girls on the bleachers, waiting for my turn to run laps or shoot hoops, I was sure they were all staring at my mannish legs. I tried desperately to cover them by pulling my shorts as far down my thighs as possible, but this did little to hide my hairy secret. I was sure they were gawking at my ginormous calves.

I wanted to be feminine and delicate like the cool girls I admired.

Even on the hottest Florida days, I hid my bulky lower body beneath sweatpants and jeans. I gathered that men liked girls with petite bodies, and my monstrous legs made me anything but petite. I wanted to be feminine and delicate like the cool girls I admired in the halls. I watched the way the guys flirted with them, pinching their tiny waists playfully and slinging their arms over their thin, girlish shoulders.

I did everything I could to be like them. I wore ribbons

in my hair like they did, making sure the color matched my outfit. I bought the chunkiest platform shoes I could find at the discount shoe store. I made my sister straighten the curls out of my hair with a clothing iron, kneeling beside the ironing board as she passed the hot metal as close to my scalp as possible. But I could never be like those girls with perfect, stick-straight bodies — not with my legs of steel.

One New Year's Eve, when I was midway through high school, my older cousin Maria stopped me on my way to the buffet table.

"Holy calves!" she said, pulling on my arm and turning me around. "Girl, you've got amazing legs."

"What?" I said, flustered, pulling down the hem of my knee-length dress.

"Seriously," she continued, flashing me a big smile. "I know so many people — girls and guys — who would kill for legs like that."

"Really?" I asked.

"Oh yeah! People do all kinds of crazy exercises to get legs as sculpted as yours. Leg lifts and squats and what not. And believe me," she said, leaning forward and lowering her voice. "Guys love girls with strong legs."

I let out a creaky laugh and slid out of her grasp. *She can't be serious,* I thought. But as she walked away, I noticed her legs beneath her tight skirt. She didn't have stick straight legs, either, but they didn't look terrible in a pair of high heels. Maybe there was some truth in her words.

After that, my idea about what a beautiful body looked

like began to change. Instead of unconsciously consuming what glossy magazines showed me about beauty and femininity, I investigated my own feelings about the female body. Whoever said that being strong wasn't beautiful? I became less self-conscious about wearing shorts and skirts. So what if my legs were more muscular than those of your average football player? I decided there were more important things to worry about than the size of my calf muscles.

> My idea about what a beautiful body looked like began to change.

Over the years, my tolerance for these strong and curvy legs of mine turned to affection. People still stop their cars to comment on my muscular limbs when I'm strolling in my neighborhood, but I don't see the attention as negative anymore.

Once I realized all the amazing things that my strong legs allow me to do, I stopped wishing for my muscles to disappear. These legs have carried me many miles, across mountains and rough terrain. With my muscular legs, I can swim across lakes, pedal across continents, and dance until morning.

I'll never have the lithe build of the cool girls I looked up to in middle school, and there are some outfits that I cannot pull off because of my bulky frame. Some men might be intimidated by a woman with a body like mine, sculpted and strong, but those are not the men I am interested in. I can't change the fact that I was born with a muscular body, nor do I want to.

Instead, I have decided to lean into my body type. These days, I never think twice about wearing a pair of shorts, a tight skirt, or a short dress. In fact, the shorter the better.

I am no longer afraid of appearing strong, nor do I associate strength with manliness. It is my hope that my children will grow up in a world that celebrates the beauty in women's strength. My curvy legs are one of my many strengths, and I love showing them off to the world.

— Carmella de los Angeles Guiol —
Chicken Soup for the Soul: Curvy & Confident

Name something that bothered you in the past that got better.

_____

_____

_____

What is bothering you now?

_____

_____

_____

Can you imagine it will get better, too?

Circle one: YES NO

Embracing My Uniqueness

*The one thing I've learned is that
stuttering in public is never
as bad as I fear it will be.*
~John Stossel

M y grandfather stuttered, as did my uncle. My brother stuttered, too. And, at forty-one years old, I still stutter.

I'm fine with it now but that wasn't always the case.

It wasn't too terribly difficult the first couple of years of school. In fact, I don't recall being made fun of at all, although there was a great deal of curiosity about my abnormal speech.

In the second grade, one of my classmates asked me why I talked funny. With a straight face, I told her that I had a piece of meat lodged in my throat, which caused my words to get stuck. She believed me.

Several years later, she asked me if I still had that meat stuck in my throat.

To this day, stuttering can be difficult, in more ways than one, to explain.

Less than one percent of the world's population stutters; however, there was only one stuttering kid in first grade at Jeter Primary in Opelika, Alabama, and that stuttering kid was me.

Kids love recess, naps, and show and tell, and I was no different. Recess and naps came easy, and in spite of my speech disorder, I still took part in show and tell just like all the other kids. I just did a whole lot more showing than I did telling.

At the time, I didn't like being different. I felt that I stood out for all the wrong reasons.

It's never easy being a kid, but it's especially tough when you're different. Just imagine the pain, shame, and embarrassment of not even being able to say your own name. I would often give fake names when meeting new people, because it was easier. It was not uncommon for me to be Jason or Mike, Chris or Kevin or just whatever sounds I was confident I could say at that particular moment.

Most little boys are shy when talking to girls, but I was downright terrified. I can probably count the number of times on one hand that I talked to a girl in elementary school. Years later, many of those same girls told me they thought my stuttering was cute. I wish I'd known that then.

As I got older, some kids started getting meaner and the teasing started. Unfortunately, I let it bother me. I shouldn't have, but I did. I put more stock in what they had to say rather than being thankful for the overwhelming majority of kids who treated me with kindness, respect and compassion. In hindsight, I know that it was a reflection of them and not me. Again, I wish I'd known that then.

I had sessions with Ms. Watson, my speech therapist, biweekly. Although challenging, my time with her was special. While in therapy, there was no pain, shame, or embarrassment. I could simply be myself and work on my speech at the same time.

Reading aloud in class was pure torture.

Class was a different story altogether. It was a constant struggle.

It was not uncommon for me to know the answers to questions, but it was quite common for me to remain silent out of fear of being ridiculed.

Reading aloud in class was pure torture. The buildup and anticipation of being called upon created more stress and anxiety than I am able to put into words, which often resulted in tension headaches.

When it was my time to read, I would lower my head, focus, and stop breathing. I would instinctively hit my thigh with my fist over and over to literally beat the words out of me, whereas other times, I would hit the underside of my desktop. This technique helped me get my words out but there was also a shadow side to it. When talking to my friends, I would often beat their arms until I finished saying what I had to say.

Could anything be worse than that? Yes, it could.

Giving an oral presentation in front of the class was the ultimate challenge, which usually resulted in ultimate shame. There was nowhere to hide. All eyes were fixed upon me as the secondary effects of stuttering stole the show. My eyes closed and my face contorted as I struggled to get out each word. There was no desk to pound and beating my leg in front the whole class was incredibly awkward.

Kids were mean and I let that bother me. There were very few days this future soldier didn't find himself crying by the end of the day. I didn't like who I was and didn't want to be me. The pain, shame, and embarrassment were too much for me to bear, or so I thought.

The funny thing, though, was that it wasn't the stuttering that caused any of the negative feelings I had, and it wasn't the bullies, either. It was my reaction to both the stuttering and the bullying.

I let it bother me, but it didn't have to be like that.

Sometime in the eighth grade, my attitude changed. I don't recall exactly when, where, how, or why, but I turned what I'd always perceived as a negative into a positive.

> **Instead of waiting in fear for the teacher to call my name, I raised my hand.**

I wasn't a star athlete and I wasn't a genius. I wasn't in the band and I certainly couldn't sing, but everyone still knew me, because I stood out, and that was a good thing. I was different and I finally embraced that difference and ran with it.

Instead of waiting in fear for the teacher to call my name, I raised my hand when I knew the answer to a question. I always volunteered to read and even used oral presentations as an opportunity to showcase my comedic talents.

I was in control and would not allow the anxiety or insecurity to control my feelings, attitude, or behavior.

In subsequent years, I'd go on to speak in front of the entire student body on multiple occasions.

Being in control eased most of the tension; inevitably, there were fewer headaches, secondary effects, and, to a degree, stuttering.

I surrounded myself with good kids and didn't overly concern myself with the occasional wisecrack. At this point, I knew it was a reflection of them and had no bearing on my character whatsoever. Besides, my own wisecracks were much better than anything they could dish out.

Self-acceptance is crucial to happiness and success in and out of the classroom. It doesn't mean we can't strive to improve upon our so-called flaws, but it doesn't mean we shouldn't love ourselves and embrace our uniqueness either.

Individuality should be celebrated, not suppressed, and certainly not mocked.

I went from a stuttering kid who seldom spoke a word to a stuttering man who now speaks for a living. Self-acceptance continues to be essential in the success I've experienced as a speaker, comedian, writer, and soldier.

My lone regret is that it didn't happen sooner.

It's never easy being a kid. It's especially tough when you're different, but it doesn't have to be.

The time to embrace your uniqueness is now.

— Jody Fuller —
Chicken Soup for the Soul: Think Positive for Kids

Chapter 2

MAKE TRUE FRIENDS

Playing Chicken

For attractive lips,
speak words of kindness.
-Audrey Hepburn

When I was in grade school I had one really great friend. We lived on the same street and liked to do the same things: bike ride, roller skate and build forts in the empty treed lots around our house.

Monica was a tall girl who had moved from the United States to our little patch of Vancouver Island, Canada. This made her a star in my eyes. Minnesota sounded so foreign, a place where magical things happened.

We became fast friends and were inseparable most of the time, almost as though we were joined at the hip. When we weren't actually together we would be on the phone talking about someone or making plans for this or that. One day in grade four, the strength of our friendship was tested.

As luck had it, that year we were put into two separate classes, something that neither of us was pleased about. We even tried pleading with our parents about the situation but it turned out that our parents were for the separation, saying that it would make us focus on schoolwork more.

I was stuck in a classroom with some of the more "popular girls." They had the best and latest clothes, toys and went on big vacations. I can remember being so jealous of them sometimes, and it would only make me more lonesome for Monica. I tried to be nice to them, thinking perhaps that once I got to know them they would not be as bad as I imagined, but they just looked down their noses at me. I knew most of them were brought up in the same neighborhood and that would have been another reason why their bond was so strong, but it didn't take the sting out of the rejection.

> I was stuck in a classroom with some of the more "popular girls."

Which is why what happened on the schoolyard took me so off guard.

Monica and I were down on the bottom playground where a balancing beam stood two and a half feet from the ground. We liked to play a game called Chicken on the beam. We would each walk in from one end, meet in the middle, and see who could knock her opponent off the beam with her arms. We were having a great time trying to knock each other off when we heard "Well if it isn't Laurel and Hardy." Jennifer, the most popular girl in the school, always referred to us like this. I had to ask my dad who they were and he told me about the classical comedians of the black and white era of American television. I looked them up. They were two men who dressed up in suits and did slapstick comedy. One was tall and lean — that was in reference to Monica, and the other was short and stout — in reference to me. The names at first didn't bother me at all because I didn't understand the insult, but once I knew who they were and watched some of their acts I got what Jennifer was laughing about.

Monica and I stopped our mock "Chicken Fight" and hopped down. "What do you want, Jennifer?" I asked, knowing full well she hated being called by her full name. She came over to me and smiled; her friends circled and crowded around.

"We've noticed you," she said, pointing at me. "We want you to join our group. There is a sleepover this

> "You are invited, but only if you give up your friendship with Laverne here."

weekend at Stacey's house and you are invited, but only if you give up your friendship with Laverne here." She finished pointing at Monica.

I started to get really angry by this point; she had just insulted us again about our height differences and insinuated that Monica was somehow flawed. Why would she think I would give up my best friend for her and her band of ridiculous girls that clung to her every word? I wanted a friend of equal footing, not some girl who wanted to be the queen reigning over her subjects.

I looked at Monica and tears were welling up in her eyes; she had this look on her face that said I should do it and she would not be mad. Monica turned to leave. I looked at Jennifer who, by now, had a victorious grin.

"Wait!" I called out to Monica. "Where are you going?"

"What do you mean? You can't be friends with me if you want to be friends with them."

"Who says I want to be friends with them?" My smile grew larger as I saw the shocked expressions on Monica's face and on the faces of the other girls.

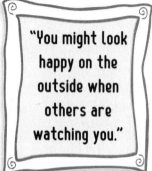

"You might look happy on the outside when others are watching you."

"I would not take a thousand of them over our friendship. They have no idea what true friendship is; if they did they would never have asked the question," I told Monica. The smile was restored on her face.

I went over to where Jennifer was standing. "You have made me realize something. You aren't happy. You might look happy on the outside when others are watching you, but that is only so they won't know how lonesome you truly are. There is nothing like a good friend to turn to when things get tough, or when you have something great to celebrate. Hopefully sometime soon you will find this out."

Then Monica and I left them standing there, silent, and headed back to class. The popular girls had played Chicken, and they had lost.

— Tracie Skarbo —
Chicken Soup for the Soul: Think Positive for Kids

The Gift of Lost Friendship

You have enemies? Good.
That means you've stood up for something,
sometime in your life.
-Winston Churchill

When most people look back on middle school they remember their teachers and their best friends. But what I remember most is one person who isn't even my friend anymore. Lots of people will give you the gift of friendship, but this person gave me an even bigger gift. She gave me the gift of no longer being my friend. I know that sounds strange, but let me explain.

My heart was pounding as I climbed onto the school bus on the first day of middle school. I adjusted my backpack as I looked for a place to sit. My eyes landed on two girls sitting next to each other. They smiled at me and patted the seat adjacent to theirs.

"Hey!" the blond said. "My name is Heather. What's yours?"

"Rachel..." I stammered. Normally I'm not shy, but I barely knew anyone and was anxious to make new friends.

"Nice to meet you," said the brunette. "My name's Jessica."

I sat down on the hot vinyl seat and faced the girls. I looked at my Converse All Stars and frowned. Why hadn't I worn more stylish shoes?

"Do you live around here?" I asked.

"Over there," said Heather, pointing left.

"I just moved here from across town," explained Jessica.

It turned out we had first period together and we became friends. We ate lunch together, hung out at the park and had *Smallville* marathons in Jessica's room on weekends. We became the three musketeers. But our friendship wasn't without its faults.

> She had an "I'm-the-boss" personality that demanded attention.

Jessica made Heather and me laugh. She was very fashionable and we'd go to her for make-up and clothing advice. But she had an "I'm-the-boss" personality that demanded attention. She always had to be in charge.

One time, the three of us went to the mall. Being the preppy one, I wanted to go to Abercrombie & Fitch.

"Abercrombie, are you kidding?" Jessica said, rolling her eyes. "I'm not setting foot in there. We're going to Rave."

Not wanting to argue, I followed her into Rave, my eyes lingering on the door to Abercrombie.

"This skirt would look great on you," Jessica exclaimed. "Try it on!"

"I don't like it that much..." I said.

Jessica gave me a death glare so I made my way to the dressing rooms.

I ended up buying the skirt. I spent fifty dollars on a skirt that I didn't even like, just to make Jessica happy.

> I spent fifty dollars on a skirt that I didn't even like, just to make Jessica happy.

Throughout sixth grade, this was how it was. If Jessica went somewhere, Heather and I went there too. We had little fights, but nothing major. That summer was filled with sprinklers, lemonade, midnight trips to the pool and afternoon tanning in the backyard. But when seventh grade started, things were different.

Heather and I became Jessica's sidekicks. If Jessica wanted to go ice skating, Heather and I were obligated to come. If we were busy with other plans, it didn't matter. We had to come or she would say we "didn't care about our friendship." If Jessica was mad at me, Heather always took Jessica's side. When she was mad at Heather I did the same thing for fear of being yelled at by Jessica. Even though most fights were just minor misunderstandings, they usually ended with Heather or me apologizing and praying for Jessica's forgiveness. Then we'd mumble to each other about how ridiculous the latest fight was.

As time went on, I found I was behaving as a pretend version of myself just to please Jessica and to keep her from being mad at me. She complained I was different when I was around other people, when in truth I was being myself. I was always afraid she'd get mad at me for saying something that I wouldn't normally think twice about.

I was obligated to take Jessica's side even when I didn't agree. For instance, one time she got in a fight with a girl named Leslie and she expected me to be mad at Leslie too. When I told her I had no reason to be mad and that Leslie was my friend, Jessica didn't speak to me for three days.

I found I was behaving as a pretend version of myself.

Then, summer came around. Jessica invited Heather and me to go to Cape Cod with her. I decided to go to Florida with another friend instead, and Jessica got angry. When I came home, Jessica was gone. I went to camp and didn't hear from her.

One hot day, my phone rang and the caller ID glowed "Jessica." If I answered, I'd be yelled at. If I didn't, Jessica would get even madder. I flipped open the phone.

"Hey... How are you?" I asked.

"Fine," Jessica replied curtly.

"Is something wrong?" I questioned, biting my lip.

"Why do my other friends call and you don't?!" she demanded.

My heart raced. I remained silent for fear I'd say something wrong. Finally, I took a breath, "I'm sorry.... I've been at camp and in Florida. If you wanted to talk so badly, why didn't you call me?"

"You don't care enough to call me!" Jessica exclaimed. "I can't be your friend anymore if you don't care."

I needed to tell her the truth. I took a breath and whispered, "Jessica, I'm afraid of you. You're fun to be with, but you're intimidating. I never know when you're going to get mad at me." My voice shook. "It's hard to have a friend who's always angry — there, I said it. I'm sorry if it hurts your feelings. I want to work things out but I thought you should know how I feel."

The line went dead. She'd hung up on me. Heather had a similar falling out with her within weeks.

I sometimes wonder what life would be like if I hadn't told the truth. But telling the truth is never a mistake, and that's what Jessica taught me. Without knowing it, Jessica showed me that real friends listen to what you say and care how you feel. Real friends are there for you through the toughest times — they don't cause them. Real friends respect who you are and encourage you to be yourself, rather than asking you to be who they want you to be just to please them. Lots of people will give you the gift of friendship, but once in a while someone will give you the gift of lost friendship.

— Rachel Joyce —
Chicken Soup for the Soul: Teens Talk Middle School

Finding Friendship

Don't wait for people to be friendly,
show them how.
—Author Unknown

In middle school I was the shy, quiet girl who always did her work, sat in the back of the class, and never raised her hand for fear of giving a wrong answer. My shyness was a problem when it came to meeting new people, but I had a small group of friends who I had grown up with, and I believed they would always have my back. Emily, Vicki, and Michelle were my three best friends in the whole world; they were also my only friends.

Vicki was the leader; she took it upon herself to always invent games and take charge, and she absolutely hated anybody standing up to her. Put simply, she was bossy, and if something didn't go her way, she wouldn't hesitate to fight.

Michelle was Vicki's sidekick, and she was much more passive. She followed Vicki around like a puppy dog, and went along with whatever she said.

Emily was quiet and not as bossy as the others, but she

was also more assertive than I was. She never picked fights with anybody for disagreeing with her, and she never had anything bad to say about anybody. I trusted her the most of my three friends.

> I finally saw my friends' true colors, and it felt like a slap in the face.

I was in sixth grade when I finally saw my friends' true colors, and it felt like a slap in the face. I had just finished gym class, and I was walking to the cafeteria with Vicki, Michelle, and Emily. It was time for lunch, which was my favorite part of the day.

We walked in as a group, with Vicki and Michelle in front, while Emily kept pace directly behind them. I brought up the rear, walking slowly and silently. Without warning, the three sat down at a table nearest the entrance, and I suddenly noticed that there were no empty seats for me to sit in.

"Very funny, guys," I said softly, hoping they would move to another table. The one where they had chosen to sit was already full with a group of boys that I barely knew.

"Can you make room for me?" I asked, and I could already feel the flush of embarrassment creeping up my cheeks.

"There's no room," Vicki said simply, looking me straight in the eye.

"Can't we just sit at a different table?" I pleaded. I felt humiliated. I was being abandoned by my best friends, my only friends.

"No. We're sitting at this one. You should just walk faster

next time."

"Yeah," Michelle piped in.

I looked desperately at Emily, my last hope, but she stared down at the sandwich in her hands instead of meeting my gaze. She acted like I wasn't even there.

The hurt and embarrassment of this betrayal was enough to shatter what little self-esteem I had, and I could barely make my voice audible, much less keep it from breaking.

"Wow, thanks guys," I choked. I had tried to make it a sarcastic, biting comment, but I couldn't maintain my composure. I wanted them to feel a fraction of the pain I was feeling, I wanted them to regret this. But Vicki had already moved on and was starting a new conversation with Michelle.

I shuffled away from the table, holding onto my lunchbox for dear life. I refused to let myself cry, but I couldn't stop my face from turning what must have been an unsightly shade of red. I glanced at every table I passed, skimming each one for a single friendly face. I just needed someone to sit with, just for today. Sadly, this was the moment I realized I really  had no other friends. There was nobody else I could sit with. I finally made my way to an empty, dirty table in the back of the cafeteria.

I wished desperately that someone would join me, and I angrily wondered why my friends couldn't have simply sat at this empty table.

Halfway through lunch, a teacher walked over to my table.

I wondered frantically if I had done something wrong to draw his attention. I didn't want to get in trouble.

"Hey, Brianna," Mr. Hickey said to me kindly. His voice was soft and comforting, but that didn't stop my anxiety. "Did you and your friends have a fight or something?"

I shook my head vigorously, "No, we're fine."

"Then why are you sitting all alone?" he seemed concerned, and a small part of me was thankful that somebody was taking notice, but I didn't dare say anything about my friends.

"I just felt like sitting here for a change, I guess. I don't really know." I shrugged and bit into my sandwich like it was no big deal.

He nodded slowly, and started turning away. "Okay, well, if that's all. Enjoy your lunch." He looked back at me over his shoulder, but only for a moment, before a group of boys shooting milk out of their noses drew his attention and he was gone.

The next three days followed a similar pattern, only it soon became a race not to be the last to the table. I was desperate, but somehow, I was always last. For three days I sat by myself at the dirty table in the corner. Mr. Hickey didn't approach me after that first day, but I never missed his glances in my direction.

One day this pattern was broken. I was sitting alone at my table, like always, when a small voice asked, "Can I sit here?"

Startled, I looked up to see a girl named Stephanie who I only vaguely knew. She had ridden the same bus as me the year before, but other than that I had never really had much contact with her.

"Yeah, sure," I said, eagerly making room for her.

Suddenly, lunch didn't seem so miserable. We talked all period, and my heart felt like it was going to burst. Stephanie's act of kindness was hugely important to me, and I have never stopped feeling entirely grateful to her. I also didn't miss Mr. Hickey's quick smile as he watched us from over his shoulder.

My entire table, once empty, was almost completely filled.

The next day, it wasn't just Stephanie who joined me for lunch. Emily came over, as well as three other girls who were friends with Stephanie. A few short days later, my entire table, once empty, was almost completely filled.

Finally, there was only one person missing.

"Can I sit here?" Vicki asked softly.

I looked at her for a long moment, and Stephanie opened her mouth to deny her.

"Yeah, there's a seat next to Michelle." I cut in.

Vicki scurried over to the indicated seat, and Stephanie turned to me, asking why I had let Vicki join us.

I had no answer other than sometimes a little kindness can go a long way. I had learned a lot over those few days, and finally I saw who my real friends were. Stephanie, who was practically a stranger, had seen me when I needed help, and she was the only one to come to my rescue when my "friends" abandoned me. Now I want to reach out to others, to spread kindness and love, just as Stephanie did for me.

—Brianna Abbott—
Chicken Soup for the Soul: Just for Preteens

Stephanie reached out to Brianna and sat with her at lunch. That started a trend, and lots of kids joined Brianna at her table.

Is there someone who seems lonely who you could reach out to?

_____

Have you noticed someone who might make a good friend for you, but you've been afraid to try?

Circle one: **Yes   No**

What's your action plan?

_____

Identify someone who seems lonely:

_____

Decide how you'll reach out to that person:

_____

What do you think the result will be?

_____

Growing a Spine

*A lot of people are afraid to tell the truth,
to say no. That's where toughness comes into
play. Toughness is not being a bully.
It's having backbone.*
~Robert Kiyosaki

I don't remember important things from middle school: student council elections, school dances, most of algebra... but I'll always remember the little things, like a single bench in the gym locker room, because that's where I started the slow process of growing a spine.

It was seventh grade, and it was supposed to be the turning point of my middle school career.

Sixth grade had been awful. I hadn't wanted to go to optional sixth grade at a middle school at all — I'd wanted to stay in sixth grade at my elementary school with my best friend in the universe, Jesse. But Mom insisted, and so I went forth to the middle school along with the more "mature" students from my elementary, girls who cared more about nail polish and gossip than reading and pretend. In elementary school, Jesse and I had scorned those girls as being shallow and unoriginal. In sixth grade I found myself trying to fit in with those same girls.

I gossiped and schemed my way into a small group. There were four of us: Tina, Ashley, Katie, and me. Tina was the ringleader, our Queen of Hearts. We spent most of our time trying to get on her good side, and neurotically worrying that she was talking about us behind our backs. And we were right to stress. Not unlike the Queen of Hearts, Tina's whims were subject to change, and she chose a different group member to ostracize every month. (Only instead of "Off with her head!" it was more like "Off of our exclusive lunch table!")

You might ask, "Why would you want to stay friends with someone like that?" I often asked myself the same question. What it came down to was fear. I was a spineless little wuss who avoided confrontation whenever possible and had relied on Jesse for protection throughout my entire childhood. The group offered me the same protection — a place to sit at lunch, someone to walk with between classes. Being friends with Tina was better than being confronted by her. Plus, I told myself, it would only last a year. In seventh grade, Jesse would come to my school, and everything would go back to normal.

And that day had finally arrived. I sought Jesse out and knowledgably led her to our homeroom.

> **I was a spineless little wuss who avoided confrontation whenever possible.**

While we waited for our new class assignments, Jesse introduced me to her friend Alice, an unsure-looking, fast-talking girl who she'd met in sixth grade. I greeted her enthusiastically, telling her, "Maybe you'll be in the same class as Jesse and me." Jesse was the smartest girl I knew, and I had no doubt that she'd get into the accelerated class with me. If Alice was smart too, we'd almost be enough to have a group of our own!

Papers were passed out that held our schedules and class assignments. "7X," I recited my class name proudly.

"7X," Alice read.

"7Y," said Jesse, crestfallen.

I swear, for a moment my heart stopped beating. "That can't be right," I said. "Look in the upper right hand corner. It should say 7X."

She shook her head, and I grabbed the paper from her. Sure enough, she was in a different class with a different schedule. I would be stuck in Cliqueland without an ally for two more years.

We ranted angrily for the rest of the class — Jesse and I for obvious reasons, Alice because she would not know anyone in the accelerated class. "Don't worry," said Jesse confidently. "Val's my best friend. She'll take care of you."

At that point, I probably gulped.

You see, our first class was Art, a room with huge double desks. In our group, we had an arrangement. Whenever the class had to pick partners, I was always with Katie, leaving Tina free to sit with the marginally cooler Ashley. So I found myself hovering in the back of the Art room, staring at two empty chairs. Would I abandon Katie and risk Tina's possessive wrath or would I sit with Alice, who I didn't even know?

I took a deep breath and sat beside Alice.

I power-walked into the hallway when that first class ended, but Tina caught up with me anyway. "So are you, like, dumping Katie now?" she asked.

"Of course not!" I said. "I can be friends with both of them."

That was easier said than done.

Alice threw off the number of girls in our class from eight to an uneven nine, and so the partner issue came up over and over. When history projects were assigned, Katie moved her desk expectantly toward mine. "Maybe we can ask Mr. P if we could have a third person," I said.

"He said only two people," said Katie, with an air of "there's nothing we can do." So, being my typical spineless self, we left Alice alone.

After a few weeks of trying to bounce between Alice and the group, Tina decided that it was time to be more forceful. "Why are you hanging out with Alice, anyway?" she demanded, as we walked to gym class. "She doesn't even like you. She's just using you because she has no friends."

I walked on to the locker room, to the gym bench where our group always changed clothes, fear clenching up my stomach, my heart pounding. Nothing would ever change. I asked myself why I even bothered to help someone like Alice, who I hadn't really bonded with. We probably, I rationalized, had nothing in common.

Then Alice dumped her gym bag on our bench and Tina

said, "There isn't really room for you."

I stood silently, watching Alice pull her gym bag off the bench and leave, the words "She'll protect you" repeating insistently in my head. I listened to Tina laugh, watched Katie smirk, and it hit me — it didn't matter if Alice and I never got close. The girls in my group were not the type of people I wanted to be.

> The girls in my group were not the type of people I wanted to be.

I wish I could tell you that I confronted Tina then and there, that I called her all kinds of deliciously vicious names and declared my alliance to Alice, once and for all. But I don't think people go from being completely spineless to speaking their mind in a matter of minutes. A transition like that takes time. But I can tell you that I never chose the group over Alice again.

The funny part is: once Tina saw that I wouldn't back down, she abruptly decided Alice was cool. We were a group of five for the two months before Tina moved (oh happy day!) to Pennsylvania.

A few weeks after the gym bench incident, Alice called me with a homework question. We somehow got onto the topic of books, and realized we loved all the same authors. We talked for hours.

Ten years later, we're still friends.

— Valerie Howlett —
Chicken Soup for the Soul: Teens Talk Middle School

The Birthday Party

It's nice to be important,
but it's more important to be nice.
—Author Unknown

I love parties. I always have. I love planning for them, making the invitations, planning the games and decorating my own cake. The only thing that I don't like is deciding on the guest list. When I was in grade school my mom would tell me the maximum number of friends that I could invite and it was always a number too small for my list.

I also liked all different kinds of people. I never quite fit into one of the many little groups at my school, so I just kind of floated around, accumulating friends from various cliques. There was an "in" crowd made up of the cool kids who had the power to rule the school — if a cool kid wore two different colored socks to school one day, everyone thought it was great. But if an uncool kid did the same thing, the other

> I never quite fit into one of the many little groups at my school.

kids would turn away in disgust. It made getting dressed in the morning a very scary thing. Without knowing exactly what the rules were, I never knew if I would inadvertently cross the line of "uncoolness."

Shannon was one of my friends who seemed to unknowingly break the rules all the time. I don't know why she was targeted, but people found it acceptable to make fun of her. Shannon was a nice girl and wore pretty clothes, but was somewhat overweight and didn't talk much. She was picked on a lot. Whenever there was an odd noise or smell in the classroom the kids would giggle and point at her. Shannon never said anything, but it made me feel sick inside and I was relieved that the kids hadn't pointed at me.

One year, to celebrate my birthday, my mom told me I could have a party at our house. I struggled for days deciding on which girls to invite to keep the number within the specified limit. Once I had chosen all the names, I made the invitations and handed them out to my friends at school.

"Why did you invite her?"

"Why did you invite her?" asked one of my cool friends when it was discovered that I had invited Shannon. She insisted that I had made a big mistake and pressured me to tell her not to come. There were other people I could add in her place who would be more acceptable. I wasn't sure what to do; I liked Shannon, yet I was afraid that I would become the target of the girl's ridicule if I admitted that Shannon was my friend. I knew the right thing to do, but I struggled with the fear of having to live with my decision.

I decided not to say anything to Shannon and let the invitations stay as written, but I worried about what would happen. The day of my party, both Shannon and my other friends came, and all that happened was that we had a lot of fun together. It was not unlike other parties I had been to and none of the things I had worried about came to be. More parties and events followed that one and the memory of it was whisked away almost as quickly as the colorful paper plates on which we ate our cake and ice cream. In fact, it was many years later before I thought about that particular party again.

I was at my high school twenty-year reunion when a beautiful, slim, very professional-looking woman walked up to me. She said, "Lindy, I am so glad you came tonight. You're the reason I am here."

"Oh?" I replied, not recognizing her face at first. She pointed to her nametag that read, "Dr. Shannon Chatzky." We hugged and laughed and caught up on the years that had passed since we had last seen each other. She was now a wife, a mother and a doctor!

Then she told me something that stayed with me. She said, "Grade school was awful for me. I hated to

> "I will never forget that you invited me to your party."

get up each morning, dreading the ridicule that would come each day. I struggled all the time with thoughts of ending my life. I came tonight to thank you for being my friend. You made my days bearable and I will never forget that you invited me to your party."

Shannon cherished the memory of that birthday party from so many years before. It was important to her that I had welcomed her into the fun, and it was a day when she felt accepted and part of a group. She talked about the games we played and the cake we ate, remembering all the details. For me, it was just a simple party, one I hadn't even remembered. But for Shannon, it was a party she would never forget. And now, neither will I.

— Lindy Schneider —
Chicken Soup for the Soul: Just for Preteens

Chapter 3

DO THE RIGHT THING

I Pledge Allegiance

I like to see a man proud of the place in
which he lives. I like to see a man live so
that his place will be proud of him.
—Abraham Lincoln

The first day of junior high school! Excitement crack-
led in the air. My mom dropped me off at the curb,
and I practically skipped onto my brand new cam-
pus. Everywhere, kids were greeting each other,
grinning and laughing. I waved at familiar faces and called
out, "Hi!"

It was weird, but after just three months, everyone looked
so different — taller, with new haircuts, new clothes.

I had P.E. for first period. I didn't mind it that much,
since it meant I'd get it over and done before the heat of the
afternoon. I was weirded out by the locker room though. It
even smelled funny — stale and musty. We all bustled around
each other, shoving our backpacks beneath the benches, trying
to figure out the combinations on our new locks. I smiled at
the girls next to me and they smiled back.

In a far corner of the room, a speaker squawked on. "Good morning, Woodrow Wilson Junior High School students! Welcome to the first day of a fabulous new school year. We'll begin with the Pledge of Allegiance."

I tugged my gray gym shirt over my head and my right hand immediately rested over my heart. Around me, other girls froze in place, all of us looking towards the flag draped near the speaker.

A few tears came to my eyes. Every time I did the pledge, I thought of my grandpa. He had died almost a year before, but I still missed him every single day. Grandpa served in World War II and the flag had very special meaning for him. Even if we heard the pledge or the national anthem on TV, we stopped everything and saluted. He would get this distant look in his eyes, like he could see all the way to India and China where he loaded bombers during the war. It had made him proud and sad all at once.

The principal finished reciting the pledge. The other girls unfroze and resumed dressing. The day continued, full of reunions and excitement and groans as we confronted our first homework assignments of the year.

The next morning in the locker room, I noticed something odd. Some of the girls talked through the pledge and

> I was the only girl in the whole locker room who did the Pledge of Allegiance.

continued to change clothes. The morning after that, even fewer paused to place their hands over their hearts. I looked at the gym teachers' cubby and was shocked that they talked and laughed through the pledge, too.

By the second week of school, I was the only girl in the whole locker room who did the Pledge of Allegiance. I stood out. That's when the comments started.

"What do you think you're doing?" sneered one girl.

"The pledge," I said.

"What's wrong with you? We don't have to do the pledge anymore." She tossed her hair over her shoulder.

"Yeah," another girl chimed in, "there's no one to make us do it!" They shared a triumphant grin.

I had known some of these girls since second grade, but now it was like I didn't know them at all. It wasn't just their hairstyles and bodies that had changed over the summer. Something else had changed, too.

It felt so wrong to be hiding like that.

The next morning, I hid in a bathroom stall to switch clothes. When the pledge started, I faced a graffiti-covered metal door as I mouthed the words. I couldn't see the flag. My stomach clenched in a great big knot. It felt so wrong to be hiding like that.

I kept hiding for the next week, and it felt worse every single day.

The other girls left me alone, and that should have made me glad. It didn't. Instead, I felt like I was betraying the memory of my grandpa. He risked his life fighting for that flag. I rarely saw him cry, but when he'd hear the song "I'm Proud To Be An

American" by Lee Greenwood, tears would fill his eyes. Now, tears were filling my eyes as I cowered in a bathroom stall. I wished that I could go to the teachers for help, but they didn't seem to care about doing the pledge, either.

I cared. I cared a lot.

I spent a weekend gathering up my nerve and practicing what I would say. By the time Monday came, I was nervous, but also calmer than I had been in a long time because I knew I was doing the right thing.

I changed into my gray gym clothes right away and was standing by my locker when the principal began morning announcements. The pledge started and I put my hand over my heart.

A girl nearby slammed her locker shut and looked over at me. "Why are you doing that?" she asked. She didn't sound mean about it, more like she was confused.

"My grandpa fought in World War II and he died last year," I said. "I'm doing it for him."

She blinked. Embarrassment flickered over her face and she looked away. "Oh," she said.

Over the next few weeks, more girls confronted me, thinking they could bully me about the pledge. I gave them all that same answer. Eventually, they stopped asking.

I came to realize something. These kids thought they were rebelling against something they were forced to do in school. The fact was, every single girl in that locker room probably had a family member in the military at some point. With a Navy base nearby, some of them even had enlisted dads.

I never inspired other girls to do the pledge along with me. That was okay. They made a choice; I made mine. It was enough that I stood there, in the open, to say those words. I was doing it for Grandpa, but more than that, I was doing it for myself.

Grandpa raised me to be proud to be an American, and that pride didn't stop because I was in seventh grade.

— Beth Cato —

Chicken Soup for the Soul: Think Positive for Kids

SPEAK UP
STAND UP
STAND PROUD

My Bad Reputation

A lie may take care of the present,
but it has no future.
~Author Unknown

E very day after school my parents made me sit and write… "I will not tell a lie! I will not tell a lie!" I repeated the sentence over and over until my hand felt as if it might fall off.

It was the middle of third grade and I am not sure what had gotten into me. I lied for no reason at all and about the dumbest things. I lied that I had eaten all my dinner, when

> I lied for no reason at all and about the dumbest things.

in fact I buried it in the bottom of the trashcan. I lied that I had made my bed, when clearly by entering my room it was obvious I had not. I lied that I had brushed my teeth; with a quick check it was obvious the toothbrush wasn't even wet. My lies were not hurt-

ing anyone, but for some reason I felt the need to say things that were not so.

My parents tried everything to understand why I felt the need to make up stuff. I was grounded; I was watched closely so that I did what I was supposed to do, I was talked to and lectured while they tried to get to the bottom of where my poor behavior was coming from.

Was I looking for attention? As the middle child, maybe I wanted attention I wasn't getting. I soon realized the new attention I was getting was horrible. I was labeled a liar and my parents did not trust me. I promised to stop telling lies.

A few days later my sisters and I were invited to spend the weekend with my aunt. We all loved the times we were invited to Aunt Kim's house. She did not have children of her own so she spoiled us with her time. Not much of a cook, she gave us the perfect food for a third grader — hot dogs and macaroni and cheese. She took us roller-skating at a park with a long path and she was an amazing artist so arts and crafts were a big part of our afternoons. She had cool pencils, erasers and other supplies that any young girl would love to get her hands on.

The day finally arrived for the fun to begin. As my parents dropped us off and visited a few minutes they made it a point to tell my aunt to keep an eye on me and to not let me fall back into my world of silly lies. I was embarrassed and angry but when they pulled out of the driveway I forgot all about their lecture.

Then it happened… sometime that day someone took one of Aunt Kim's good art erasers and rubbed it across the entire top of the TV. The eraser ruined the shiny finish on the TV's casing. When Aunt Kim discovered the destruction all three of us were called into the TV room and asked to confess. Nobody did! Boy was she mad. I had never seen that side of her. She told us how disappointed she was and that someone would have to take responsibility. Again, nobody said a word. The next thing I knew she was on the phone with my parents and they were on their way to pick me up.

It had to be me! I was the liar. No amount of protesting could convince any of them that I had not committed the crime. I was taken home and sent to my room for the rest of the day. I begged and pleaded my case, but no one listened. Why would they? I had been telling lies for the past few weeks so of course it had to be me.

No amount of protesting could convince any of them that I had not committed the crime.

I stayed in my room the rest of that day thinking of all the things my sisters were getting to do without me. I was labeled a liar and now I sat alone with nothing to do. My parents finally let me out for dinner. And then there was a knock at the front door! Aunt Kim was standing there. I could not believe it. I was sure she and my sisters were already watching a movie from her big collection. Why had she come? It turns out my younger sister finally felt guilty! She confessed that she was the one who rubbed the eraser on the TV. Aunt Kim had come to get me. I was invited back!

Funny, I don't even remember being mad at my sister. I learned a valuable lesson about lying. No matter how big or small your lies, once you are labeled a liar earning trust takes a lot of work and time. I promised myself right then and there to never lie again.

—D'ette Corona—
Chicken Soup for the Soul: Think Positive for Kids

Service with a Smile

> Judgments prevent us from seeing the
> good that lies beyond appearances.
> –Wayne W. Dyer

It was an early Saturday morning, about 5:30 a.m. My mom called to me. "Austin, get up! Time to go and serve the homeless!" I dragged myself out of bed.

I started serving the homeless when I was eight years old. I didn't know these people would make such a big difference in my life.

Two Saturdays a month I go to the church and help get things ready for breakfast. When the gate is opened, people come rushing in to get coffee, juice or milk. They take their seats while breakfast is prepared, and then we begin to serve. We each grab two plates and carry them down the line as the plates are filled. Each person receives two pancakes, a scoop of eggs, hash browns, and two sausages. I walk to the tables where the people are sitting and set the plates before them. I always make sure to smile. After I've served them, I ask if they need anything else and bring them whatever they ask for.

Some say thank you, some don't, but I don't care. I'm there to serve them.

When I first started serving I was a little scared. Some of the people were wearing clothes with patches on them and shoes with holes in them. They were not that

> **When I first started serving I was a little scared.**

clean and their teeth were yellow or missing. At first I stayed close to my mom most of the time, but after I got to know these strangers I realized that they were nice, friendly people. And the inside of them was often nicer than the outside. I started talking to my new friends and realized that there was no reason to be scared. After serving for a few months, I started to look forward to seeing the same people each week.

Take Cowboy. He always puts me in a good mood. When I see him, he always says, "Austin! How are you?" I've often heard him say that I am a really hard worker. This makes me feel really good inside because I know I'm making a difference in someone's life. There's a guy named Larry who has a lot of piercings and tattoos — even tattoos on his face! I would feel a little scared if I saw him on the street and didn't know him, but now that I do know him I've realized that he's a very nice guy. He even works at a church and helps others, too.

Then there's Curtis. He's a really big guy. Every time I see Curtis, he is very talkative. He always has a big smile on his face. Curtis has a friend named James. James is even taller and bigger than Curtis. When I first saw him, I thought, "Whoa! Is he a nice guy or not?" He looked really tough. But as soon as

I met him, he said — in a deep, deep voice — "Hello! What's your name?" I knew that we would be good friends.

> **The past two years have made a big difference in my life.**

All of these people make my day much better. When I don't see one of them, I wonder if they are okay. The past two years have made a big difference in my life. I do this because it is the right thing to do. When I serve people I want them to know that someone cares for them and that they matter — they are not just "homeless" — they are human beings. Serving makes me happy, but even more importantly, it teaches me to love and respect others and helps make the world a better place to live.

— Austin Nicholas Lees, age 10 —
Chicken Soup for the Soul: Volunteering & Giving Back

Easter in Ruins

Sometimes being a brother is even better
than being a superhero.
~Marc Brown

I was eight years old the first time that I felt sympathy for my sister. I was a terrible brother. I didn't do anything outright dangerous to my sister, but I teased her mercilessly, generally made her feel terrible, and certainly did not contribute anything positive to her self-esteem.

I didn't really care. It was part of who I was. I didn't know, then, that it was also shaping who she was.

Then along came Easter, one of our favorite holidays. Not because we were devoutly religious and we understood what the holiday actually meant — we were kids, after all — but because that mystical

I didn't do anything outright dangerous to my sister, but I teased her mercilessly.

white bunny came and left us baskets full of candy, toys, and useless green filling.

My sister and I thought we were special because the Easter bunny would always hide our baskets. I'd asked my friends at school and barely any of them ever had to find their Easter baskets. They were just there waiting for them when they woke up.

How boring.

Easter morning arrived and it was time for us to spring into action.

"Michelle," I whispered, peeking through the brown plastic door that separated our rooms. It latched closed with a small magnet that worked for approximately two days after my father had installed the door.

"Michelle," I said a little louder this time. "Wake up. It's Easter. We have to go find our baskets."

She rolled over in bed and pulled down the covers just far enough to peek her eyes over her blanket at me, like a crocodile looking up from a murky swamp.

"Michelle!" I whispered more intensely. "Let's go!"

I pushed the plastic door to one side of the doorway and slipped into my sister's room, sat down on the bed, and shook her hard.

Even at age six, my sister was a late sleeper. She had absolutely no desire to stumble out of her bed at the crack of dawn to open presents, hunt for Easter baskets, or do anything other than close her eyes and fall back to sleep.

I, however, was impatient. And a terrible brother.

"Now!" I shouted before slapping my hand over my mouth. The last thing I wanted to do was wake up our parents, only three rooms away in the small first floor apartment.

After a few minutes, my sister finally relented, pulled herself out of bed, and started looking for her socks.

"Mom and Dad are still sleeping," I warned her as we crept through our rooms and out into the kitchen. "If we're quiet, we can find our baskets without waking them up."

It didn't take long for me to find my basket. It was sitting right behind my father's favorite recliner, overflowing with chocolatey goodness and it was obviously mine because it contained the latest issue of my favorite wrestling magazine.

My sister continued searching in every room while I dropped my bounty off at the kitchen table and started separating candy into categories: Chocolates, jellybeans, malted chocolate eggs.

It had to be at least twenty minutes before I looked up from my potential sugar rush displayed on the table to see that my sister was still looking for her basket.

"I can't find it," she said. She looked upset. "I looked all over. Can you help me?"

I had no interest in helping my sister find her Easter basket, so I started to head back to my loot on the table.

"Please?" she asked again. "I can't find it."

I decided to help my sister find her Easter basket, but don't get the wrong idea. It wasn't because I felt sorry for her. Not at all. It was because I'd now been issued a challenge. I had a mission and a case to solve. The Case of the Missing Basket.

"Okay," I said. "Let's keep looking."

We started searching through the cabinets where my mom kept her pots and pans.

By now, our parents were awake. Dad headed straight for the bathroom, while Mom tossed her gray, wool robe over her shoulders and made a beeline for the coffee maker.

"Looks like the Easter bunny came!" she said, looking at my treasures covering the kitchen table. "You found them already? He must not have done a very good job hiding this year."

"I found mine," I said and nodded towards my sister standing in the doorway between the kitchen and the living room.

Mom spun around and looked across the room at my sister.

"Where's yours, Michelle?" she asked.

And that's when my sister started to tear up. She wasn't fully crying yet. Michelle was as tough as sisters come, even at six years old. It was as if her six years of dealing with all my teasing had already hardened her to this cruel, cruel world.

"Let's keep looking," Mom said, grabbing my sister's hand. "I'm sure it's here somewhere."

My sister smiled and pulled our mother into the living room, where they started looking under the couch cushions and behind our television.

Nothing.

"You know," Mom said suddenly, "we haven't looked in any closets."

She pointed across the living room to the hallway closet with the doorknob that never quite held the door closed.

Michelle shot across the room and swung open the closet

door. She got down on her knees and started rifling through the shoes and bags and mismatched gloves on the closet floor.

Nothing.

I heard her sniffle just slightly as she sat back on her heels, defeated.

"Look up!" I said. "Up above the jackets!"

Mission accomplished.

"My basket!" she yelled. "Mom, my basket is up on the shelf! Can you get it?"

Our mother smiled and pushed her way into the closet just far enough to reach up into the dark recesses above the coats and plastic bags and snowsuits hanging below. Way up on the shelf where we usually kept our car washing bucket and soap was my sister's Easter basket.

"Here you go, honey," she said, as she handed Michelle her basket, too excited (or relieved or tired) to notice anything strange before passing it off. "I told you the Easter bunny didn't forget you."

And that's when it happened.

My sister. The rock. The tough girl that I, until that day, had never seen break down. Michelle started crying. And when I say crying, what I mean is tears streaming down her face into a messy puddle in her Easter basket.

My sister's Easter basket was empty. Not completely empty. But it was empty all the same. All that remained were the half-chewed remains of Kit Kat wrappers and nibbled pink Barbie boxes. The only thing still intact? The fake green grass in the bottom of the basket.

Mom called my dad into the room and pointed to my sobbing sister and her sad little basket. "Mice!" Dad said as he started tearing the closet apart. "I'll get them..." That was the last thing we heard him say before the sound of winter jackets, a dustpan, and the vacuum hitting the floor overwhelmed the room.

By now, Michelle had stopped crying. She'd dropped her basket on the floor, wiped her tears, and retreated to her room.

"Just leave me alone," I heard her say as Mom followed her to the door. "Leave! Me! Alone!"

That was my tough little sister, the one I had trained to be strong and not reveal her feelings through my relentless teasing. She wasn't going to shed any more tears in front of us.

> I suddenly felt something I'd never felt towards my sister before.

But as I sat at the kitchen table flipping through the March issue of my magazine, snacking on an Almond Joy, I suddenly felt something I'd never felt towards my sister before. I felt sad for her. I felt it go through my body like a chill. I felt exactly what I thought she felt. Complete and utter sadness. Only, I wasn't nearly as tough as she was.

I dropped my magazine, reserved one Reese's Peanut Butter Egg (my favorite) for myself, and put the rest of my candy back in my Easter basket on top of the green plastic grass.

I walked slowly into my sister's room, where I found her sniffling quietly under her covers. "I'm sorry, Michelle." I said quietly. Maybe even too quietly for her to hear it.

I took one last look at the fully stocked Easter basket and then I left the whole thing right there at the foot of her bed.

I went back to the kitchen to get my magazine, and then got back into my bed to read.

And then, through the thin plastic door between our rooms, I heard the faint sound of candy being unwrapped.

I smiled, lay back on my pillow, and put on my headphones.

That was the last time I ever saw my sister cry.

— Scott Neumyer —
Chicken Soup for the Soul: Think Positive for Kids

A Tough Decision

I would prefer even to fail with honor than
to win by cheating.
-Sophocles

When I was in my first year of junior high I was an average student. I got all A's and B's and had many friends. I had one secret, though: I cheated. I cheated starting from about halfway through the fifth grade, which was when the work started getting difficult. I didn't want to get held back or fail the grade and have to see all my friends move on without me. So, I did the only thing I could think of — I cheated. The real fact was I just couldn't pay attention and learn the new subjects. I cheated all through the rest of fifth grade, even on the TAKS (Texas Assessment of Knowledge and Skills). And it didn't stop there.

As I moved into sixth grade I was making new friends and leaving old ones behind. I seemed like a regular sixth grader. None of my friends knew I cheated, mainly because I cheated off their papers too. As junior high went on and teenage drama started entering my life, I found it harder and harder to pick up and learn the few things I did learn. So I began cheating on everything. It became more difficult to cheat, since the teachers began to put me in the front of the class, possibly to watch me more closely. Because of this, my grades started to drop quickly. Some of my teachers asked if everything was okay. Of course, I just said I hadn't been sleeping well, which was the only excuse I could think of at the time. When I thought things couldn't get harder, I started getting picked on by the other kids.

I thought my life would never get cleaned up and I would never go to college or be a zoologist (my dream job). That's when I started to consider telling someone. The first person I told was my best friend, Sherry. She was really smart and she was the person I told all of my secrets. Of course the one thing she said was, "Elizabeth, you need to stop. You need to tell the teachers and clean this all up." Of course, I really didn't plan on telling because I was scared. I thought that the teachers would never look at me the same way again, that they'd never be able to trust me.

I was gravely wrong. I continued cheating all the way through the semester exam. But after that I got seated by the kids who also failed, so I couldn't cheat off the smart kids. My grades plummeted. I didn't know what to do, so I went back to Sherry. She told me the exact same thing again, but this time it meant something to me. I took it to heart and thought, "My teachers will forgive me. It's not like they're going to hold this against me forever."

That time I was right. Sherry and another friend, Taylor, who I also told, finally convinced me to come clean. It was the longest Thursday of my life. Finally, the dreaded fourth period came around, which was when I had Mrs. Burnum, my science teacher. She was the teacher I felt most comfortable around, so she was the one I had decided to tell. Right after the bell rang, I walked up to her and asked if I could talk to her outside. At that point I was sweating and shaking. She asked what was wrong.

I just poured everything out. I explained why I had failed the mock TAKS test. I emptied everything I had bottled up. Mrs. Burnum said that the teacher I took my mock TAKS with, Mrs. O'Conner, should hear my confession. Mrs. O'Conner, who taught reading and language arts, was the strictest teacher I had. Mrs. Burnum accompanied me to her classroom and, with a reassuring nod, eased me into telling Mrs. O'Conner. She nodded while I was explaining and when I finished I could tell she wasn't happy. But all Mrs. O'Conner said was, "Elizabeth, you know cheating is wrong. It is never the right decision. Why did you do it?"

They were proud of me for telling them.

First, I sighed with relief that I wasn't getting detention, and then I explained how I would have most likely gotten held back and hated to see my friends move on without me. I just couldn't let that happen.

Mrs. Burnum gave me an unhappy look and said, "Elizabeth, if you had told someone, you know you would've gotten help."

I nodded, fighting back tears.

The next thing my two teachers did surprised me. They told me they weren't happy, but they weren't angry either. They were proud of me for telling them, even though they were shocked and surprised I'd been cheating for an entire year. But they also said I wasn't giving myself enough credit — they didn't believe I could've gone a whole year without doing any of the work myself.

Again, they were right. It turned out that as I had been looking at the other kids' papers, I had been learning.

Mrs. Burnum and Mrs. O'Conner ended up holding a conference with my parents about the whole matter. After the conference the teachers started helping me a little bit more and I ended up catching up on things quickly. I only cheated one time after that and I got caught. But that time it wasn't because I didn't understand; it was because I didn't finish my science review the night before. The teacher told Mrs. Burnum and I got detention for it, but I learned my lesson and I haven't done it since.

> I am happy I confessed, otherwise my life would still be miserable.

I am still in sixth grade and still learning and preparing for the TAKS test coming up, but now I do my own work and I no longer have wandering eyes. I am happy I confessed, otherwise my life would still be miserable. Sometimes when I get home my mom will ask me, "Haven't done any cheating today, have we?" And I will always reply, "Mom, you know the answer." Whenever I hear teachers talk about kids who cheat, I am proud to no longer be one of those kids. The decision to tell my teachers and my family the truth was difficult and frightening, but ultimately it was the right thing to do.

— Elizabeth M. —
Chicken Soup for the Soul: Just for Preteens

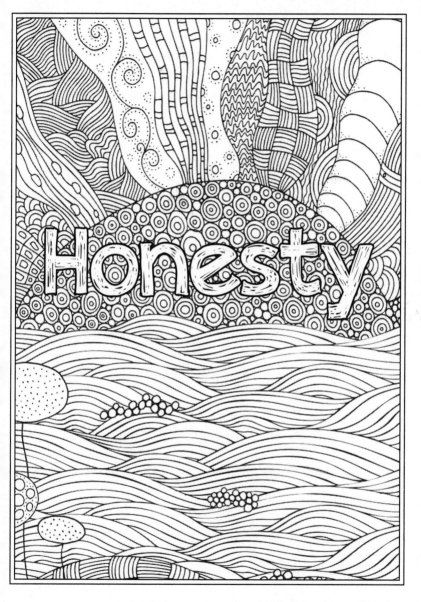

Party Invitation

*A man has to live with himself,
and he should see to it that
he always has good company.*
–Charles Evans Hughes

I was excited. I had been invited to go to my friend's birthday party. Tori was not my best friend, but she was in my class and we did stuff together. And I liked to go to parties. I asked my mom and she said I could go, so I told Tori that I'd be there.

And then, two days later, my very, very best friend called. She and her family were going to Disneyland for the whole day. She invited me to go with them. Disneyland! I loved Disneyland so much. I really wanted to go… more than anything. I ran to ask my mom if it was okay. That's when my mom reminded me that Tori's party was on the same day. She said I couldn't change my mind just because something better came

> She said I couldn't change my mind just because something better came along.

along.

I was mad. So mad. Disneyland was my most favorite place in the whole world and I loved to go there... and I especially liked going with my best friend. My excitement about going to the birthday party was gone. Tori's party would be okay but not as fun as a whole day at Disneyland and besides that, Tori wasn't even my best friend. I begged my mom. She said no. I cried. I sulked. I pouted. My mom still said no. What I wanted to do wasn't nice. It wasn't right.

I couldn't get her to change her mind. I tried every excuse I could think of. My mom explained to me again — once you accept an invitation to something, you can't change your mind and go to something else just because you want to do the other thing more. That isn't nice. She asked me to think about how I would feel if someone did that to me. If someone had said they'd come to my party and then, because something better came along, they changed their minds and didn't come, how would I feel? I thought about

> In spite of the fact that I had not wanted to go, I had a great time!

it. Although I didn't want to admit it, my mom was right. It would hurt my feelings if someone did that to me. Although I didn't want to, I told my best friend that I wouldn't be able to go to Disneyland with her.

So my friend and her family went to Disneyland and my mom dropped me off at Tori's party. I did not want to be there. But something interesting happened after I got there.

In spite of the fact that I had not wanted to go, I had a great time! We did stuff that was fun and different. We watched a movie that hadn't come out in theaters yet; we were the first people to see it and that was pretty amazing. There was a make-your-own pizza contest. We each got a piece of dough and then there were all of these toppings to choose from. We all got covered in pizza dough, cheese and toppings. You're supposed to take a present to the birthday person and we all did. But Tori's mom and dad had a special present to give to each of us too! That was so cool.

When my mom came to pick me up I didn't want to leave. After we got home I told my mom all about the fun things we had done. She was so glad that I'd had a good time and she told me that she was proud of me for understanding why you can't just dump someone because something better comes along. Not only did I love the party and have a great time, but I learned an important lesson. My mom was right... as usual.

— Barbara LoMonaco —
Chicken Soup for the Soul: Think Positive for Kids

Tennis Anyone?

Character is doing the right thing when
nobody's looking. There are too many
people who think that the only thing
that's right is to get by, and the only
thing that's wrong is to get caught.
~J.C. Watts

One summer when I was about ten years old, my brother and I received a wonderful gift — tennis rackets and balls. We had never had the opportunity to play tennis, so this was exciting. However, there was one problem — the small town we lived in did not have a tennis court.

One Saturday morning my brother said, "Hey, I've got an idea. Let's take our tennis rackets and balls to the school and hit the balls against the school building."

"Great idea! Let's go," I agreed, not realizing what a lesson we would learn before the experience was over.

When we got to the school ground, no one was around, so we began hitting our balls against the side of the two-story brick building.

"I'll hit it the first time," my brother suggested, "then you hit it the next time. We'll hit it back and forth to each other."

So we began taking turns hitting the ball, getting more confident with each stroke. Actually, we became pretty good at returning the ball and we were hitting the ball higher and faster each time.

Suddenly, the unthinkable happened—the ball got out of control and went crashing through one of the upstairs windows.

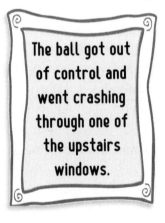

The ball got out of control and went crashing through one of the upstairs windows.

We looked around and no one was in sight—except—there was an old man sitting on a porch halfway down the block.

Quietly, I asked, "Now what should we do? Our ball is inside the school."

"Well," my brother responded, "no one will know whose ball it is. And no one saw us, except that old man down there. And he probably can't see this far."

"He probably doesn't know who we are anyway," I added.

"Let's go home," my brother suggested.

"Okay," I agreed. "Should we tell Mom and Dad?"

"I don't know," my brother answered.

As we picked up the rest of our balls and headed for home, the decision as to whether we should tell what had happened was carefully weighed out. But that decision was made for us the moment we walked into the house.

Our mother was always in tune with her children. "What happened?' she asked as soon as she saw us.

"Well," my brother slowly began. "We had a great time hitting the tennis balls against the school."

Then I interrupted, "until we hit it too hard and too high and it went right through the school window."

"Oh, my goodness!" my mother exclaimed. After a short pause, she continued, "You will have to tell your father as soon as he gets home."

And so we did. As soon as he walked in the house, we both hurried to him and poured out our story.

His response was typical. "Well, today is Saturday and tomorrow is Sunday, but first thing Monday, I will call the school janitor and see what we need to do. You will probably have to pay for the window."

We had two agonizing days to wait until our dad got home from work on Monday.

He looked very somber and we were sure that the news was bad. We were sure that every penny we had saved would have to go to fix the window.

Then my dad smiled. "Well, I talked to the school janitor and he was surprised to hear from me. He had been sitting on his porch watching while you two were playing tennis on Saturday. He saw the whole thing and was surprised when I called to tell him what had happened. He said many windows had been broken, but we were the first ones to call and admit that we were responsible. He said the school budget allows for

> "I am proud of you kids for having the courage to tell us what happened."

window repair, so we will not have to pay for the window, but he was glad we called."

He could see our relief as he continued. "I am proud of you kids for having the courage to tell us what happened."

I'm not sure at that moment whether we were happier to be able to save our money, or to hear our dad say he was proud of us. But either way, we discovered that there is always someone who sees what we do and we might as well confess our mistakes and be willing to take the consequences.

— Shirley M. Oakes —
Chicken Soup for the Soul: Think Positive for Kids

Chapter 4

GO AHEAD AND TRY IT

The Spelling Bee

*The best way to conquer stage fright
is to know what you're talking about.*
-Michael Mescon

S pelling was my favorite subject in fourth grade. Every week I memorized my new words, and by Friday I was prepared to take the spelling test. I usually got all the words right. My teacher, Mrs. Casazza, wrote "100%" and "Excellent!" on the top of my paper, and when she handed it back I felt so proud.

In the desk behind me, Donna Slocum would lean forward and whisper, "What did you get?" and I'd show her my test paper. "Again?" she'd ask, with a hint of jealousy in her voice.

One day Mrs. Casazza announced to the class that we would have a spelling bee on Thursday, the day before our test. "It will be a review for those who are having a difficult time remembering their words," she said.

Oh, no, I thought. Last month when I had to stand up in front of the class and give a book report, my arms shook so badly that it was hard to read my paper. I was overly conscious of the twenty-seven pairs of eyes on me, and all I wanted was to run back to my seat. A spelling bee would be even worse. I wouldn't have a paper to read from!

After lunch on Thursday, Mrs. Casazza told us to line up by the board, and she explained the rules. "Say the word, spell it, and then say it again," she said. "Be careful not to repeat any letters."

One at a time, she pronounced a word for each student to spell. Two boys made mistakes right away and had to sit down. With clammy hands, I waited for my turn. After the girl next to me correctly spelled her word, Mrs. Casazza called my name and said, "Your word is 'echo.'"

"Echo," I started. The sound of my own voice startled me. "E."

> Everyone was looking at me, waiting for me to say the next letter.

Then my mind went blank. I couldn't think. Everyone was looking at me, waiting for me to say the next letter. But I couldn't see the word in my head. All I could see were the other kids, and they all had their eyes on me. My face got hot. I swallowed hard. What came next? Was it K? No. It sounded like "k" but it wasn't, was it? It was "c."

"E-C-H-O," I spelled slowly. "Echo."

Oohs and aahs came from the kids beside me. "You repeated the 'E'!" Donna pointed out.

"She's right," Mrs. Casazza said. "You'll have to sit down."

I looked down at the floor and made my way back to

my desk. Although I was relieved that I was no longer in the spotlight, I felt like crying because I knew how to spell the word.

Afterward, Mrs. Casazza said, "The spelling bee worked so well, and we all had so much fun, that I've decided to have a spelling bee every Thursday."

It worked so well? We all had so much fun? Every Thursday?

I didn't want another spelling bee! I was afraid that I'd mess up again. And sure enough, when the next Thursday came, I did. I started spelling my first word, and then I suddenly became conscious of everyone in the room staring at me. I stood silent a long time, unable to finish the word. The room was quiet while Mrs. Casazza waited. Finally, she sent me back to my seat.

"Just imagine everyone's wearing nothing but their underwear."

I dreaded the spelling bee so much that I didn't want to go to school the following Thursday.

"What's wrong?" my mother asked. "Are you sick?"

I told her about the spelling bees, and how each time I messed up my first word and had to sit down.

"But you're a good speller!" she said. "You do so well on your tests!"

"I can't spell when they're all looking at me!" I said.

"Oh, so that's the problem," she said. "You've got stage fright. I heard of an easy way to get rid of that. Just imagine everyone's wearing nothing but their underwear."

I laughed. "Their underwear?"

"Try it," she said. "It will remind you that they're no different from you."

Mom seemed sure that her trick would help me, so I went to school believing it would.

During the spelling bee, my first word was "piece."

"Piece," I started. "P." The feeling that everyone was staring at me began to creep up again, but I remembered what Mom had said. I pretended my classmates were dressed only in their underwear. I must have smiled a little. My head cleared and I concentrated. Now did the word start with P-I or P-E? I knew this. We'd learned that there is a "pie" in "piece."

"I-E-C-E," I said. "Piece."

"Very good," Mrs. Casazza said.

Hooray! I did it once, so I knew I could do it again. And I did, again and again. Throughout the year, I even won a few spelling bees. That was just the beginning. My mother's trick helped me with every speech and book report I had to give. I stopped thinking that I couldn't get up in the front of the class. Of course, I could! With a little imagination, anyone can!

— Mary Elizabeth Laufer —
Chicken Soup for the Soul: Think Positive for Kids

Discovering My True Self

*If you hear a voice within you say
"you cannot paint," then by all means
paint, and that voice will be silenced.*
−Vincent van Gogh

I looked out at the smiling faces packed into the school auditorium. Flashes from cameras lit up in all directions. The applause filled my ears. I had done it, I had really done it.

Just a few months earlier, I would never have pictured

> I would never have pictured myself acting in a play in front of two hundred people.

myself acting in a play in front of two hundred people. "Not for a million dollars," I would have said. But when the time came, I got up on stage and faced one of my greatest fears — and discovered I could do more than I ever gave myself credit for. I found a new person inside me, a much more daring, outgoing person who had been hidden all along, just waiting for the opportunity to emerge.

If not for my teacher, Mrs. Sather, I might never have found that opportunity.

In the first and second grade, I was extremely shy. I had friends, but it just wasn't in my personality to be very outgoing, even when I knew someone well. I was even quieter with strangers, and so I wasn't very good at meeting new people. I was afraid I would do or say something wrong, so usually I just smiled and listened to other people's conversations.

I did well in school, though, and I loved to write. I would escape in my writing, where I could be myself and never have to worry about what other people thought of me. In my stories, I was never shy.

My second grade teacher, Mrs. Sather, always encouraged me to write more. She told our class to go after our dreams and dig in with both hands. I think she was one of the first people to see my inner strength.

One day, she announced that our class was going to perform a play she had written, a take off on *The Wizard of Oz.*

"I'll begin to cast everyone tomorrow," she said. "I need someone who is not afraid to be on stage in front of a lot of people to play the lead part of Dorothy. Anybody want to try?"

A few excited hands shot up — mine, of course, was not one of them — and Mrs. Sather smiled. "We'll talk more about it tomorrow," she said.

The three o'clock bell rang, and my classmates slowly

filed out with their *Beauty and the Beast* backpacks and *Lion King* lunch boxes, chattering about the play.

I lingered at my desk, loading up my backpack, and was one of the last to leave. "Dallas," Mrs. Sather called to me. "Will you come here for a minute, please?" Confused, I nodded and hurried to join her at her desk. *Was I in trouble?* I grew even more worried when she said, "Maybe we should wait for your dad to come pick you up. He might want to hear this, too."

As if on cue, my dad walked in, his tall, lean frame filling the doorway. "Hi, Dal, how was your day?" he asked as he helped me slip my backpack over my shoulders.

"Um, fine," I managed to croak out through my dry throat.

"I was just telling the class about the play we'll be performing in the spring," Mrs. Sather related. "It's going to be a take off on *The Wizard of Oz*, and Dallas, I was thinking you would be perfect for Dorothy. But I was surprised you didn't raise your hand when I asked who was interested in the part."

Me, the lead? Was she crazy? I was terrified just thinking of standing on stage in front of all those people. I hoped to grab a small part where I could sit in the background and watch everyone else sweat over lines in front of all those pairs of eyes.

"W-well," I stammered, "um, I thought it seemed really hard, and I was never very good at talking in front of lots of people."

"Oh, Dallas, you're great at memorizing things, and you have such a sweet personality. Perfect for Dorothy!" She paused. "Of course, plenty of girls would love the role, and I could get somebody else…"

Mrs. Sather gazed into my eyes as if seeing my inner self locked away inside. "But I'd love for you to give this a try for me. I had you in mind for Dorothy while writing the play! If you really don't want to, though, I won't make you. It's your choice."

My mind was spinning faster than the merry-go-round on the school playground. Mrs. Sather, whom I loved and admired, wanted *me* in this role. She believed in *me*. My gaze shifted across the room and stopped on a poster I had never noticed before. It showed a shooting star and read, "If you reach for the stars, you might at least grab a piece of the moon."

It was time to throw off my shy cloak and show the world who I really was.

I realized it was time to throw off my shy cloak and show the world who I really was. I looked Mrs. Sather right in her sparkling blue eyes and said, "Okay, I'll try."

Fast-forward through five months of practicing, set building, line memorizing, and costume creating. We were ready. I knew my lines, blocking, songs — and the rest of the cast's lines, blocking, and songs. Still, I was as nervous as I had ever been. My knees shook. My heart pounded like I had just run a mile. I proved to myself that I could do it in practice, but could I prove it to everyone else when it really mattered?

"It doesn't matter how you do tonight," said Mrs. Sather, as if reading my thoughts when she came backstage for a final check. "You have already shown yourself how wonderful you are. That is the most important thing."

I smiled because I knew she was right. I proved I could take chances, be daring, and have fun doing it! At the end of the play, when the audience stood and applauded, I knew they were not just cheering for my performance that night, but for the performances they knew would come in later years because of my newfound confidence.

— Dallas Woodburn —
Chicken Soup for the Soul: Inspiration for Teachers

Alice and Snowball

No act of kindness, no matter how small,
is ever wasted.
—Aesop

O n my twelfth birthday my mother handed me a square box. "Jamie," she said, "this is something you've wanted for a long time."

My heart beat fast as I opened the box. Out popped a fluffy, white Poodle puppy! I let out a whoop. "Thank you, Mom! I'm going to name her 'Snowball.'"

My mother smiled. "That's a good name," she said. "Now a few things: pets come with responsibility and since this is your dog, you will have to feed her, walk her, and clean up after her. Is that understood?"

"Yes, Mom," I replied.

I set to training Snowball right away, having her walk by my side on a leash. She didn't do it perfectly but I knew she would in time. I decided to take her for a short walk down a nearby, quiet lane.

As we turned into the lane, we saw an old woman sitting

in her yard. When we passed by, she called out, "Is that a new dog? I know all the dogs in the neighborhood but I've never seen this one before. My name is Alice," she said, as she came toward us on the sidewalk, dragging an aluminum canister on wheels behind her. She collapsed onto a chair near her gate, gesturing for us to come in. "It's not easy for me to breathe," she wheezed. "That's what this machine is for." I tried not to stare.

"What is this little one's name?" she asked.

I picked up my puppy and placed her on Alice's lap. "Her name is Snowball and mine is Jamie," I replied. "I just got her for my birthday today!"

"It's very nice to meet you Jamie and Snowball, and a very Happy Birthday to you," Alice said. Soon Alice had lost herself in snuggling Snowball. With Alice's eyes closed, I felt it was okay to study her breathing machine. It reminded me of something out of a science fiction book. When I looked back at Alice, I saw her clutching and patting the calm dog and softly humming to her. As I watched, I saw tears roll slowly down Alice's cheeks.

"What's the matter?" I asked.

She said, "I used to have a Poodle years ago. Holding your dog brought it all back."

"Why don't you get one of your own?" I asked.

"I'm too old for a dog," she replied.

I just sat quietly because I could not think of anything to say.

"Well," she said, smiling, "I guess it's time to give you

back your dog. I do so love a little dog to snuggle with. You two will visit me again now, won't you?"

"Of course," I said, as Snowball and I walked away from her down the lane. But I was thinking I would never go back there. I didn't want to see her again with her old lady smell and her scary breathing machine.

I lay awake for a long while that night. I felt torn because even though I didn't want to visit the old woman, I knew that it would be the right thing to do. She was sick, alone, and old— older even than my own grandmother, who was pretty old! And Snowball seemed to comfort Alice so much.

> I knew that it would be the right thing to do.

The next morning I hooked Snowball to her leash and we set out for her morning walk. I found myself taking a turn into the lane where Alice lived. Maybe we would find her out in her yard.

—B.J. Lee—
Chicken Soup for the Soul: Think Positive for Kids

Part of the Team

Teamwork is the fuel that allows common people to attain uncommon results.
~Author Unknown

*I*n 2003, my family decided to move from our home in Los Angeles to Toronto, Canada. My parents were both originally from the East Coast (Ontario and New York) and they really missed their parents and siblings, not to mention the seasons. They also wanted to move my sister and me out of L.A., which was just not as family-oriented a culture as they wanted. I was not sure about it. I knew I would miss my friends and the warm weather and year-round sunshine, not to mention the pure fun that it was living in the Hollywood Hills. I didn't know how I would like Toronto but it turned out that I did really take to it once we got settled in. And one of the things I loved most turned out to be hockey.

Before we moved, I had only been on skates once in my life, at a classmate's birthday party. I remember really liking the sensation of gliding around the ice, but that was about it. Once we were in Toronto I asked my parents if I could join the local house league to see how I liked it. I remember the night my dad took me out to get my equipment. Man, there was a lot to buy — skates, shoulder pads, shin and elbow pads, pants, helmet, stick, etc. And it took a while to put it all on too, but I was excited to try it out.

We had thought that the first evening was going to be a practice. When we got to the arena we found out that there aren't any practices in house-league hockey. So, the very first time I played I found myself right in the middle of a game! Crazy. But I was open and willing to try.

I'd always been pretty athletic. In Los Angeles I played baseball, football, tennis, lots of kickball at school, golf... you name it. But hockey was different. I was trying to play this brand new game, balancing on super-slippery ice, while teetering atop a thin metal blade. Holding the stick was new too, although it did give me something to lean on. Anyway, my hockey coach sent me out on my first "shift" and the very first thing I did was fall flat on my back. I got up quickly, took a couple of strides on my skates and about two seconds later fell again. I fell so much that game I actually got a penalty because I kept running into the referee, even knocking him over a couple of times.

I must have fallen about a hundred times during that game.

I must have fallen about a hundred times during that game... but I also started to figure out the game and actually got involved in quite a few plays. I didn't get a goal, but I did take a couple of shots. When I came off the ice my mom and dad were right there with concerned looks on their faces. To their surprise, I yelled, "I love it! I think I've found my game!" Everyone laughed, but I meant it.

After that night, I was hooked. I immersed myself in the sport, watching all the NHL games on TV that year, rooting for the Leafs, of course, and watching Sports Centre every morning before school. I became a fanatic! The thing that made me improve the most, I think, was the fact that the neighborhood where we lived had so many kids. There was a game of road hockey going on pretty much every day after school. We got a hockey net and the kids across the street had one too. We'd put them out on the street and within minutes, we would have a pick up game going. This would last until my mom would have to call me repeatedly to come in for dinner.

The following year, when I was eleven years old, I tried out for the more advanced, "select" team. I never thought I would make the team... but the coach took me. He was a great coach, a mentor to me and he is still one of our family's really good friends. And that brings me to one of the best things about hockey — the friendships.

I made some really good friends through my hockey teams. And my parents made great friends too. My family and I were all new to the area, and the parents of my team, the Leaside Flames really welcomed us all into the group. Even my little sister, Julia, who got dragged along to most of my games and practices — I think she really only liked the hot chocolate — made new friends.

There were always a few other sisters at the games and they all would run around the arena, going up and down the bleachers, and cheering loudly for us whenever we needed it. It was like we all had an instant social life — traveling to tournaments, sleepovers, fundraisers, carpooling, and that really made us fall in love with Canada!

The other thing I love to do is sing and when I was twelve I joined a children's opera company. I got a solo in this big professional production of *La Bohème*. With hockey and the show and school my schedule got so crazy. One night, after performing in front of five thousand people I had to change into my hockey gear in the car as my dad rushed me to a game. I ran into the dressing room minutes before the whistle blew and right away all the guys started laughing like mad. I had forgotten to take off the heavy stage make-up they made us wear. It took a while to live that one down! And this last year I was fortunate enough to make it to the semi-finals of *Canada's Got Talent*. Not only did all my hockey friends support me in that journey, I also de-stressed from the pressure of the performances and rehearsals by playing hockey whenever I could. There's nothing better than getting completely drenched in sweat, playing a sport that completely consumes you, to really help a guy chill out.

I just graduated from high school and my school team

> The other thing I love to do is sing and when I was twelve I joined a children's opera company.

won the city regional championships. I got to score the winning goal, which was a real thrill. And I go to a performing arts high school too... not bad for a bunch of actor/singer/artist/musicians.

I am off to Queen's University in Kingston, Ontario in the fall and I plan on trying out for the team, and if I don't make it they have a great intramural program too. I look forward to getting to know a whole new hockey family.

Bring it on!

— Jack Ettlinger —
Chicken Soup for the Soul: Hooked on Hockey

Fall 100 times

Get up 101 times

Repeat

Cell Phone Madness

Everything in moderation...
including moderation.
~Julia Child

"Surprise!" was the first thing I heard as soon as I opened the door. My family and friends were all gathered together. There were colorful balloons all over the house, a big poster that said "HAPPY BIRTHDAY," and of course a cake with a number 12 candle. It was a wonderful feeling knowing that I had finally turned twelve and I might possibly get the thing I wanted most.

I saw my mom and dad coming towards me with a small package wrapped up with really nice pink paper with flowers on it. When I ripped the paper and opened the box, I couldn't believe my eyes. I had really gotten a cell phone! I ran to give my mom and dad the biggest hug ever. "Thank you! I love you guys!"

"You're welcome. We knew this was going to make you happy but we didn't only get you this because you turned twelve, but also because you are doing well in school. We expect you to keep getting good grades."

"Of course I will!" I said confidently.

As soon as I got to school the next morning I was showing off my phone and asking everyone for their number. It was cool how I got so many contacts on the first day.

It felt like I didn't even exist in that class anymore. I wouldn't pay much attention to the teachers because I was too busy on my phone. Luckily, I didn't get caught using it.

> I wouldn't pay much attention to the teachers because I was too busy on my phone.

I'm pretty sure that the teacher did notice that I stopped paying attention to her because a week later we took a test and I failed. To make matters worse, my mom had to sign the test.

It was hard to show my mom the test. She was used to seeing A's and B's on my tests. Well eventually I showed her and she couldn't believe it. She was angry but most of all, she was disappointed. Seeing her like that made me feel bad.

Weeks passed and my dad started to dislike the fact that I had a phone. We would argue every day about why phones are bad for us. He would say, "Anahy, can you please stop texting?"

"I'm not doing anything wrong, I'm just texting my friends. I don't think there is a reason for you to get mad."

"I don't mind if you text your friends, but don't do it when someone is talking to you, when you are eating, doing homework, or when we have guests. It's rude."

My mom also joined the conversation "Anahy, I have

also noticed that you never pay attention to us, your brother or sister. It's like you have your own little world now and we don't communicate as much with your phone between us."

> "It's like you have your own little world now."

I acted like they were wrong but then I started to wonder if it was true that I was being impolite.

A week later I tried going a whole day without a cell phone and it didn't go that badly. My relatives came over and it was the first time that I wasn't using my phone. Everyone noticed because they were asking me about it. It got really annoying because everyone exclaimed "Wow!" Finally you are not using your phone." That day I had so much fun because I was actually spending time with my family and paying attention to them. From that day, I had a different point of view towards cell phones.

Phones really take you away from the rest of the world. When you use your phone you move from the real world to a technological world. I'm not saying that phones are bad and not to use them, but you do have to make some time to spend with your family too and not get stuck with your phone all day. My phone took away time from my homework and from my family. It also affected my grades.

I will keep using my phone, but I have it under better control now so that it doesn't interfere with my real life.

— Zulema Anahy Carlos —
Chicken Soup for the Soul: Think Positive for Kids

Zulema stopped paying attention to the real world around her when she got her cell phone.

Have you ever felt like people were ignoring you because they were looking at their phones?

Circle one: Yes No

List three ways you can make sure you don't ignore the real world when you are using a phone or electronic device:

1. _____

2. _____

3. _____

Learning How to Kick

A positive attitude can really make dreams come true — it did for me.
-David Bailey

I went to a private school through third grade. It was far away from my house and most of the kids who went there lived in other towns. Then my parents moved me to the public school that was close to our home. I was happy to finally be in school with kids who lived nearby, since it would be much easier to go to their houses and have them over to mine.

It was a little difficult making the transition to a new school in fourth grade, since all the other kids had been together since kindergarten. Luckily, my two best friends from the private school moved to the public school when I did, so we had each other right from the beginning of the school year. It wasn't too hard making new friends either, and the schoolwork was okay, even though it was different from my old school.

The one thing that was difficult, however, was recess. At my new school, the whole class played kickball together every single day. We had never played it at my old school, so I had no idea what to do.

Every day the best kids would act as captains and pick their teams. I was terrible at kickball and would always be one of the last kids picked. Since I was very good at academic subjects like math and writing I

I was terrible at kickball and would always be one of the last kids picked.

found it difficult to be one of the worst kids at anything! But this situation continued all year. I started to dread recess, but I showed up for kickball every day anyway. There wasn't any option, since that was what the whole class played at recess.

The summer between fourth and fifth grade, I decided that I needed to do something about kickball. I couldn't go another year with recess hanging over me like a cloud every day. I confessed my problem to one of my best friends, Carlta, who was a great athlete. It turned out that I had been kicking the ball all wrong, using the front of my sneaker and trying to hit the ball with my toes. My kick had no power that way. Carlta showed me how to kick that red rubber ball with the front of my ankle, right where my leg and my foot met. That transformed my kick. I practiced all summer and I developed a strong kick that went far.

When school resumed, everyone was surprised at how

much better I played and I started being one of the first girls picked each day at recess. It hurt a lot to kick the ball with my ankle because the rubber ball really stung my skin. But it was worth it! I kicked the ball far, we scored a lot of runs, and I was finally a valuable member of my team. I loved recess from then on.

> When school resumed, everyone was surprised at how much better I played.

Unfortunately, kickball didn't continue in the middle school where we went for sixth grade, so I only had one year of being really good at recess! But I learned a valuable lesson — I could solve a problem by asking for advice and practicing what I was taught. And I am still grateful to my friend Carlta for teaching me how to kick properly.

— Amy Newmark —
Chicken Soup for the Soul: Think Positive for Kids

Chapter 5

FACE YOUR CHALLENGES

A New Best Friend

There are big ships and small ships.
But the best ship of all is friendship.
~Author Unknown

isa and I squeezed each other as tears rolled down our cheeks. She pulled away and looked into my swollen eyes. "I want you to stay. You're my best friend."

I frowned and reached for her hands. "You're my best friend too, and I don't want to leave either. But I don't have any say."

"You're moving so far away. What if I never see you again?"

"Mom promised we can call each other and have sleepovers."

Although I was only moving ten miles away, to us it felt more like a million. I couldn't imagine life without her. She was the jelly to my peanut butter. We were always together. I knew all of her secrets and she knew mine. We doubled our joys with combined laughter, and cut sorrows in half with our tears.

I didn't want to go to a different school, and I was afraid of being the new kid. With only one six-week period left of my fifth grade year, I couldn't understand why I had to change schools, but my parents insisted. I had been going to my school for five years and knew everyone there. Now, I would have to start all over with making friends.

I was afraid of being the new kid.

Life was so unfair. Why did my parents have to be so mean? Why did we have to move? Even though I loved the new house, I resented having to change schools and leave my friends behind.

"You'll like your new school," Mom said. "You'll make friends."

I didn't believe her. I curled up like a kitten on the couch and cried. "All the kids there already have best friends. I'll be a stranger to them." I buried my face in the sofa and sobbed. "I'll never have another best friend."

Mom sat down next to me and stroked my back. "Of course you will, sweetheart." Her efforts to help didn't fill my emptiness.

The entire family made piles and packed boxes over the next couple of weeks. I put my broken Lite-Brite and cracked Etch A Sketch in the trash pile with some outfits I didn't like and wanted to get rid of without Mom knowing. I didn't really play with my Barbie dolls anymore, but I put them and all their accessories in the keep pile anyway — along with my books and Lucky, my special teddy bear.

Moving day arrived. I felt important when I got to make big decisions, like where to put furniture, which drawer the silverware should be in, and what color the bathroom would be.

I jumped with joy when Mom suggested Lisa sleep over on our first night in the new home. That night we stayed up way past our bedtime talking, giggling, and eating Cheetos. We even made some prank calls and played with the Barbies — for old time's sake. We had such fun together that it made saying goodbye the next day even harder.

The night before my first day of school, I couldn't sleep. My mind wandered to my first day at my old school as a first grader. I had gone to kindergarten in Oklahoma before we moved to Texas, and although I missed my friends when we moved, the worst part was the teasing I endured. As a six-year-old, I couldn't understand why the kids had to be so mean. No one knew how much it hurt when I was called "freckle face" and "carrot top." They didn't understand how rejected and lonely I felt when they wouldn't let me play with them and when they knocked books out of my arms and laughed.

Although I did have a few special people in my life — my sister and two brothers and a girl that lived across the street — they each had other friends they played with more than me. Their friendship did diminish some of my misery from the teasing, but it didn't keep a girl from attacking me as I walked home from school one day. She hit me several times, and the only reason she stopped was because a kind adult drove by and yelled at her. She shook her fist at me and snapped, "I'll finish with you later."

Relief washed over me as she ran away, but pain and humiliation made me cry the rest of the way home.

The teasing finally died down after third grade. A few kids still made fun of me, but most of them quit. After two years of hating school and despising myself, I found enjoyment in having friends. I was even invited to do fun things, like roller skating and birthday parties. Then I met Lisa, and everything was better with a best friend. And now, I was losing her.

I lay in bed and soaked my pillow with my tears. What if I'm teased again? What if no one likes me? I didn't expect to find another friend like Lisa, but what if I didn't make any friends at all?

> What if I didn't make any friends at all?

Monday morning, I tried on four different outfits and redid my hair three times. My mom had to force me to eat. I trembled as the principal walked me down the hall, wondering how long it would be before I was teased or beat up. When she opened the door to my new classroom, everyone looked at me. Heat rose in my cheeks and my eyes widened as I tried to hide behind the principal. My stomach tumbled and churned, and I thought I was going to throw up on my favorite shoes.

"Okay everyone," the teacher said. "This is Leigh Ann, and she will be joining our class for the rest of the school year." She looked at me and smiled, then pointed to an empty seat in the last row. "You can sit there."

I tried to disappear into the wall as I made my way to the back of the class, but everyone watched me. I looked around trying to decide who was nice and who was mean. As I did, several kids smiled at me.

As the day went on, I felt accepted. No one teased me or called me names. In fact, a few even seemed interested in getting to know me better.

By the end of the school year, I had made several friends. Although none of them considered me their best friend, I had found more happiness than I expected.

> I had found more happiness than I expected.

When I returned to school for my sixth grade year, I met another new student, Jennifer. She and her family had moved to Texas from New York over the summer, and we had an instant bond — I was born in New York. We talked and hung out and had fun together.

A couple of weeks later, she invited me to spend the night. When she introduced me to her parents, she said, "Mom and Dad, this is Leigh Ann — my best friend." She looked at me and smiled.

I smiled in return and a warm sensation flooded my heart. She was right. I had a new best friend.

— Leigh Ann Bryant —
Chicken Soup for the Soul: Just for Preteens

A Not-So-Faraway Reality

*My mother's gifts of courage to me were
both large and small. The latter are woven
so subtly into the fabric of my psyche
that I can hardly distinguish where
she stops and I begin.*
–Maya Angelou, Mom & Me & Mom

In the summer of 2003, my world was ripped apart. *Harry Potter and the Order of the Phoenix* had finally been released, and I had waited all day for my mom to get off work and pick me up to go to the bookstore. When she finally arrived, she honked from the driveway, not even bothering to come inside to change out of her scrubs.

The entire drive, she listened contently to my chatter as I summarized Harry's adventures thus far for the millionth time. It was a story far removed from her reality, but she was happy I loved to read.

We parked outside the bookstore and I hurried my mom

inside. Just as we were entering, a man was exiting with a shopping bag swaying at his side. The alarm went off and we paid no mind because we were entering the store. But then we heard a man yelling at us, and we froze instantly.

"STOP!" cried a man, his pale face splotched with red as he stomped toward us. "Wait! Don't move!" he commanded.

Behind us, the man with the shopping bag was rifling through it looking for his receipt. But the man who was yelling didn't even notice him. His beady little eyes were too focused on my black mother and me.

He had made an assumption—a sick, hurtful assumption.

"Open up your purse!" puffed the man, stabbing his finger toward the worn leather bag slung over my mother's shoulder. A pin on his chest glinted in the fluorescent light. It read: Assistant Manager. The man with the shopping bag shrugged and left.

My mother recoiled. "What? Why?"

It was as if a light bulb flickered on in his mind, illuminating the narrow pathway leading to reason. The assistant manager looked at the entrance, saw the white man exiting, and then looked back at my mother. The color drained from his face. It was then he realized he had made an assumption — a sick, hurtful assumption.

"Uh, let me see your phone," he said, a poor attempt to undo the damage he had done. "S-sometimes they, uh, t-trigger the alarm." But I already saw the proverbial steam shooting out of my mother's ears.

This man had summed up my mother in a matter of seconds based on something as superficial as the color of her skin. My mother, the registered nurse, who had worked tirelessly on her feet all day attending to the needs of others and rushed home to take her daughter to the bookstore. My mother, who worked and went to school, while raising a daughter by herself, was nothing to this man but a common thief. All her sacrifices and accomplishments were nullified because this man saw only the color of her skin. And even though I knew he was wrong — so incredibly, disgustingly wrong — I pleaded with my mother.

"Please," I whimpered, but to no avail.

"How dare you!" she yelled back, her voice a thunderous roar of pure outrage. I slinked a few steps away to the table covered with the deep blue covers of the latest edition of *Harry Potter,* and my heart felt heavy. Before all of this, I only cared about what was happening in the wizarding world. After all, Voldemort was back! But reality and its frothing hatred had reared its head and seared its way through the fantasy.

At that moment, I wished I had my own wand made of gnarled wood and dragon heartstring. I wished I could cry out *Stupefy!* to send the assistant manager flat on the cool linoleum floor in an immobilized plank, wide-eyed and mouth ajar. I wished I could cast *Silencio!* to render my mother's words of truth into nothingness as if they didn't need to be said. But I was helpless and confused, caught in the crossfire.

People stopped and stared on their way to the checkout

line. Some shook their heads with disapproval. Did they care that my mother had been profiled the instant she entered the store?

Finally, a woman arrived on the scene. Her pin said Manager. She calmly asked what happened. My mother took a deep breath and explained in exasperation the injustice that had occurred. The woman looked at her employee, whose eyes had shifted downward, and then looked at my mother. She said, "I'm sorry."

The man didn't apologize.

We left the store without the book we had planned to buy. Back in the car, my mother looked at me with eyes reddened with suppressed tears and said, "I'm sorry."

We drove fifteen minutes to another bookstore. This time I didn't prattle on about Harry Potter's world. We entered the store, and I plucked the book from the display in the entryway.

But as we walked to the checkout line, I realized something had changed.

I had experienced
racism for the
first time in my
twelve years.

I had coveted this book for what felt like a lifetime, but the excitement I should have felt as soon as its velvety cover touched my hands had been diminished. In pursuit of this book, I had experienced racism for the first time in my twelve years. Before, racism was something safely tucked away within the shiny pages of textbooks. Those black-and-white pictures were of a faraway time, so far removed from my reality. But now,

I had seen it firsthand, and I had also seen my courageous, indignant, hardworking mother be the victim of it, but also its conqueror. She became my hero, capable of stopping a bad man in his tracks. As Harry Potter would say as he cast a spell to ward off evil: *Imperio!*

— Cassie Jones —
Chicken Soup for the Soul: My Amazing Mom

Scarred But Not Different

Being happy doesn't mean that everything
is perfect. It means that you've decided to
look beyond the imperfections.
~Author Unknown

When I was fifteen months old, I was burned by hot grease falling on me from an electric skillet on the stove of my parents' home. This was an accident caused by a precocious, strong-willed, or as my sisters would say, bratty child who wanted her way and wasn't getting it. In plain terms, I pulled a pan of hot grease on myself that caused first, second and third degree burns on my face, arms and chest, leaving me with permanent scars, the worst of which is having one breast. Growing up with scars was and has been all I have ever known. My body as it is now is my "normal."

Going through grade school I never saw myself as different, other than the fact that I was overweight. The boys teased me of course, and some girls did too, but my parents taught me that these kids didn't feel good about themselves so they didn't want anyone else to either. These words always helped me get through the teasing and find friends that liked me for me.

My scars followed me from elementary school to junior high school and at eleven years old I learned that not all kids are cruel. On the first day of school we found out that we would be required to take showers in the open locker room during physical education.

> At eleven years old I learned that not all kids are cruel.

This meant that I would have to undress in front of the other girls and shower with them. They would see my scars.

"Would you feel better if I talked to your teachers to see if you can take your shower after the other girls are gone?" my mother asked.

"Yeah," I said quietly. "I'm afraid they'll laugh at me."

My mother looked at me. Even though she may have been hurting for me inside she didn't let me see it. "Remember Stacie, anyone who would make fun of you because you have scars isn't worth the worry. They just do that because they think that will make them feel better about themselves." The next day my mother went to the school and met with my P.E. teacher and together they worked out a solution: I would wait until the other girls showered and went to the next class and then I would shower and be allowed to be late for my class. I was relieved. I would avoid all of the stares and ridicule that I knew would come from my scars.

But that night as I lay in bed I felt like a coward. I didn't want to be different and I didn't want to be picked on because I was allowed to do things the other girls didn't get to do. It was then that I knew what I had to do.

The next morning as I got ready for school I had a talk with my mother. "Mom, I think I might go ahead and shower in P.E. like everyone else."

She looked at me surprised. "You don't have to, honey. The teacher has already worked the schedule out for you."

I nodded, "I know Mom, but I don't want to be different because of my scars."

"I don't want to be different because of my scars."

She hugged me and said, "I'm proud of you, but Stacie, if you change your mind, you don't have to." I hugged her back. I knew that no matter what happened, my mom would always understand.

That day I dreaded P.E., not just because it meant running, but because I knew that no matter what, I was going to shower when the other girls did. "Okay girls, it's time to go in and shower!" the teacher said, blowing her whistle. The one hundred yard walk to the locker room felt like one hundred miles. I went inside the locker room to my locker and stood there, taking deep breaths. It was now or never. As I undressed and picked up my towel, I saw some of the girls looking at me. To my surprise, not one of them laughed or made fun of me.

After we showered and dressed, all of the girls in my class walked over to me and asked how I got my scars. I told them my story and one girl asked, "Do they still hurt?"

I shook my head. "No, I can't feel anything," I said, which was true — I didn't have any feeling in my scars — not then, not now. They walked with me to our next class, talking about school and boys, but none of them talking about my scars. From that day on, P.E. was not the class I dreaded... math was. I didn't worry that I was different from the others. We were all the same; we were friends.

That day is when I realized I didn't have to be different. I just had to be me, and in doing so, friendships that began then followed me into my adult life. We all finished high school together as friends, and none of them ever made fun of me for my scars or my weight. As for the boys, when any of them tried to make fun of me, I had a whole class of friends to set them straight.

That P.E. class taught me that even though my body is different, I'm not. My scars don't make me who I am — my heart does.

— Stacie Joslin —
Chicken Soup for the Soul: Just for Preteens

Still a Winner

The best teachers teach from the heart,
not from the book.
—Author Unknown

A bright red apple fell out of my knapsack and bounced against each step before landing at the foot of the stairs. I stared at the broken apple with tears in my eyes, desperately holding onto my knee, hoping to stop the pain.

"What's wrong, honey?" my mom asked, running to me where I'd fallen at the top of the stairs. I was unable to speak as I sobbed in her arms. She held me tenderly and stroked my hair. My body trembled as I blurted out my story between gasps for air.

"My knee hurts when I run, jump and play with my friends! Last week I fell down during hopscotch. Sometimes, I have to grit my teeth to stop the tears. I didn't want to tell you because you'll take me to the doctor."

Despite my protests, my mother convinced me to go to the doctor. But nothing prepared me for what the doctor had to say.

"You have Osgood-Schlatter disease. It's a knee disorder that affects athletic kids between the ages of nine and sixteen. It could create permanent damage and pain if you don't take it easy for a while. If you're having pain, it means you have to stop what you're doing and rest."

"Can I still do sports and track and field?"

"You better stop doing organized sports for now. You can participate in Physical Education class if you don't feel pain. It's not track and field season yet. Let's wait until spring and see how you're feeling."

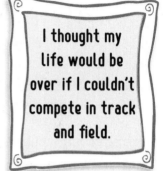

I thought my life would be over if I couldn't compete in track and field.

I sat in her office, speechless. I thought my life would be over if I couldn't compete in track and field. I was only eleven years old but I'd been the best runner, high jumper and long jumper in my school since kindergarten! I always won first prize in those three events. But the one hundred meter race was my favorite competition. Nothing boosted my ego more than my schoolmates cheering for me as I sprinted across the finish line. I said a silent prayer that God would heal my knee by spring.

When Mom brought me to school the next day, we met with my teacher, Mr. Lewis, and explained the situation. The doctor said I should elevate my leg and ice it whenever it hurt. It seemed like a big hassle, but Mr. Lewis made me feel more comfortable by sharing my story with the class. At first I was embarrassed about my injury, but soon realized it was a great way to get attention from other kids.

It was hard to stop playing with my friends and sit down, but there was always someone willing to get ice or an extra chair. The hardest part was being a spectator on the sidelines. I tried to be strong, but there were times when I'd get so mad I wanted to smash everything in the gym and curse God for doing this to me. One evening, while alone in my bedroom, I got so mad at the pain that I yelled "You stupid knee!" and actually whacked my knee with a book. Of course, that made it throb more and I had to ice it for the rest of the night.

Spring eventually came and the fateful return to the doctor was scheduled. I prayed she'd tell me everything was fine. But my hopes were shattered when the doctor explained that competing this year would put too much strain on my knee. Then the final blow hit me like a knockout punch that left my ears ringing in disbelief.

"You may never run competitively again, possibly for the rest of your life. I'm sorry."

I was crushed. I stared out the window of the doctor's office and wished I had lied to her. I should have told her my knee never hurt during sports. I should have run all year through the pain. I never should have told my parents. The conversation between Mom and the doctor grew faint as I daydreamed about winning the one-hundred-meter dash.

Nevertheless, the next day I was stuck inside, while the other kids were outside running. Mr. Lewis told me I could write for extra credit while the others practiced track and field. He had always encouraged me as a creative writer and told me

I should enter the town poetry contest that year. Every day, I worked on different poems to enter in the contest, constantly revising and perfecting the rhyme and rhythm. But the sadness of being excluded from track and field was overwhelming.

One day I was in the classroom writing when I overheard Mr. Lewis talking to the boys in the next classroom. While he explained the rules of track and field, several boys moaned and complained about participating. They were tired of running every day and wanted to quit. Until that moment, I'd never heard Mr. Lewis get so animated and loud.

"I'm ashamed of you boys! At this moment there's a girl in the next classroom dreaming about competing in track and field! She'd do anything to take your place, but because of a bad knee, she can't! You able-bodied boys should be embarrassed! You should be happy you can run every day without pain! Now get out there, start running and stop your whining!" Then he blew a loud whistle and the boys scurried outside with their cheeks flushed and their heads hanging low.

I sat in my seat in shock.

> **For the first time since this happened, I felt valued and appreciated.**

For the first time since this happened, I felt valued and appreciated. Mr. Lewis understood how much I'd lost because of my impaired physical condition. Through the tears, I smiled and thanked God for my teacher. From that day forward, I wrote my poetry with a deep conviction that I would win the poetry competition, for me and for Mr. Lewis!

That year, I did win first prize in the poetry contest of my small town in Ontario, Canada. I have Mr. Lewis to thank for pushing me to strive through difficult times.

During the last class of the year, Mr. Lewis gave everyone a special quote to take with them to ponder throughout their lives. This is what he said to me: "Kathy, people look up to you and respect you. Never lose their respect."

Before leaving the classroom for the very last time, I walked to the front and placed a big red apple on Mr. Lewis's desk.

"An apple for the best teacher in the world," I said. "Thank you Mr. Lewis. I'll never forget you."

— Kathy Linker —
Chicken Soup for the Soul: Just for Preteens

Lessons from a Nursing Home

Wrinkles should merely indicate
where smiles have been.
–Mark Twain

One chilly autumn day when I was ten my mom took my siblings and me to visit our great aunt in a local nursing home. As we entered the building, the smell of watery soup, mashed potatoes, and cleaning solution filled our nostrils. My siblings and I looked warily around the room, a large common area with a braided rug, wilting potted plants, and an old coffeemaker. Elderly residents napped in wheelchairs around the perimeter, and the only noise came from an old television. We started as an old man to our left started muttering in his sleep. An ancient woman wrapped in a yellow quilt clutched a plastic baby in her arms, singing a lullaby as if it were a real infant. Another woman stared into space with beady black eyes, nibbling on her bony fingers with toothless gums.

We gingerly made our way across the room and found our aunt asleep in an overstuffed armchair. My mom decided not to wake her, and my siblings and I breathed a silent sigh of relief. Now we could get out of this creepy room and away from all the strange old people! But then a voice sounded from our right.

> Now we could get out of this creepy room and away from all the strange old people!

"Sweetie, you have such pretty hair," said a little old lady to my six-year-old sister. "You remind me of my granddaughter."

"Oh, look at the kids!" exclaimed a woman with long white hair. "Aren't they sweet?"

One by one, the elderly people noticed us, rolled their wheelchairs closer, and greeted us cheerfully. Surprised, but not as frightened as before, we introduced ourselves and answered the many questions asked by the eager seniors. They wanted to know all about us: our names, ages, grades, and hobbies. We met Ethel, a frail woman who loved talking about her three grandchildren. Mary, a crusty but good-natured soul, made sure we all had a chair to sit in. Rose still remembered all the recipes she used to cook, and told us what it was like to be a teenager more than half a century ago. My siblings and I left the nursing home feeling like we had just made a dozen new friends.

We visited the nursing home several times after that, sometimes bringing homemade cookies or muffins, sometimes just dropping in to say "hi." Many of the seniors loved to talk and were thrilled to have so many listeners. My younger sister befriended the lady with the doll, whose name was Caroline. She was a sweet old lady who loved children and had a huge doll collection from when she was young.

We also made a surprising discovery — the old ladies loved playing beach ball! The nursing home staff taught us to stand five feet away from an old woman's wheelchair and toss an inflated beach ball right at her. To our surprise, all the ladies in the home loved to bat the ball away with their hands, feet, and even heads! They could spend hours playing catch with us — we wore ourselves out from throwing the ball long before they tired of playing!

All these events helped me realize that underneath all those wrinkles, crooked backs and missing teeth, these ladies were just ordinary, friendly people.

> Underneath all those wrinkles, crooked backs and missing teeth, these ladies were just ordinary, friendly people.

Although they looked different from me, on the inside we were very much the same. Despite my first impression, they weren't crazy or scary or strange — in fact, they had the same feelings, worries, and hopes as normal people. Just like me, they liked to laugh, talk, and make crafts. And, like me, they wanted to be loved, and to know that somebody cared about them.

The nursing home taught me that appearances are often

only skin deep, and that with an open mind and a caring heart, you can discover the beautiful person inside.

— Caitlin Brown —

Chicken Soup for the Soul: Think Positive for Kids

Chapter 6

COUNT YOUR BLESSINGS

The Boy Who Had Everything

Gratitude is an art of painting an adversity
into a lovely picture.
-Kak Sri

When I was a baby, my parents gave me anything I wanted. We would walk into a store, and anything that I wanted was mine; all that I had to do was to ask. I would play with a toy for a while, get bored, and ask my parents for a new toy. Then my dad died when I was two and a half, and I got even more stuff as my mom, friends and family gave me more and more stuff to try to make me feel better. My mom continued to treat me to whatever I wanted until I was seven and my world changed.

That was when the real estate market crashed. My mom had thought that buying houses was a good idea as a way to invest her money to take care of us. After the crash, I went from the kid who got an iPod when his tooth fell out and who had the coolest house to hang out in, to literally having nowhere to stay. My mom's best friend, my Auntie Loren, took us in until my mom could figure out what to do.

After the real estate crash, when I would ask for a new toy, or bike, or even to see a movie my mom would say "maybe for your birthday" or "I'm sorry honey, but we can't really afford that right now." I didn't know it then, but my mom had grown up in a family where money was never a problem, so this change was as big for her as it was for me. My constant requests for toys and video games were not helping my mom, who was already a widow, deal with her feelings about our new crisis — our financial situation. But I wasn't used to hearing "no" so for a year or two I kept asking.

> I wasn't used to hearing "no" so for a year or two I kept asking.

Then something happened that would change my way of thinking forever. My mom had been working really hard all year, just to pay for the necessities, like our water and power bills. When she asked me what I wanted for my birthday I said that I wanted a new video gaming system. I didn't know that it was expensive. All I knew was that my friends had them and that I wanted one too.

On my birthday, I started opening my presents, believing that I would get what I asked for. As I opened the last gift, I found two or three T-shirts and a pair of jeans. When my mom asked me what I thought, I said that I loved them, but she could tell how disappointed I was and she started crying.

I hugged her harder than I had ever hugged anyone before. I realized how hard she was working and that she couldn't afford to give me anything I didn't need and that most of the money that my mom made went to paying for rent and food.

From then on I didn't expect to get everything that I asked for. When I did, I was so excited and grateful. I think I learned the difference between what I wanted and what I needed. I learned to appreciate the toys or games I did

I learned the difference between what I wanted and what I needed.

have and to take good care of them. When I wanted a new iPod, I had to work to buy it. I got a job folding clothes at our local laundromat, and after working there for just over a month every day after school, I had enough saved up to buy that iPod.

The feeling of having truly earned something is one of the best feelings in the world. I also am lucky to have wonderful people in my life. They have made me appreciate that it doesn't matter what I have or don't have. What matters more is who I am and who I get to spend time with.

It may have been hard going through that experience, but I was able to learn some really important lessons. Now I am grateful for everything I have and I understand the feeling you get from working to earn something for yourself. People used to think I was "spoiled" because I always had everything and didn't understand how fortunate I was. Recently, my godfather

Ty told my mom that he loved to give me things because I never ask for anything and am always so grateful. I guess I've really changed.

—Jackson Jarvis—
Chicken Soup for the Soul: Think Positive for Kids

Jackson learned the difference between what he WANTED and what he NEEDED.

If you have one pair of shoes and you outgrow them, that may be something you NEED. But if you just wish you had some cool new shoes, but your old ones still fit, that is something you WANT.

What things do you NEED?

_____

_____

_____

What new things do you WANT, but you don't really need?

_____

_____

_____

Opening My Eyes

Live as if you were to die tomorrow.
Learn as if you were to live forever.
–Mahatma Gandhi

My mom homeschools me. No — travelschool is a better word for it. She likes to go on lengthy trips with my two younger brothers and me, sometimes for up to four months at a time. My brothers and I hop from school to airport to hotel. We've been around the world and back again, from Australia to France to China.

It's really cool, because we can just say "Okay, why don't we go to New York City this weekend!" and off we go. It's much better to have your mom teach just you and your brothers than having to worry about bullies and mean teachers. However, we have to work really hard at our homework to keep up with everybody else. Even though we're not in school, we write in a journal every day and study as hard as we can. We are taught the entire regular school curriculum as we travel (math, reading, writing, spelling, etc.) but that's not all we learn, either.

When I go to countries all around the world, from Thailand

to Brazil, it always amazes me how poor people are. In these places, there are people who have no electricity or running water. Clothed in rags, their worldly possessions only include a tiny hut and perhaps a pig, although they can always afford a smile and a friendly wave. You can see their teeth as they smile — you know they probably have never heard the word "dentist." It makes me feel guilty that they have to work hard every day to survive, while I think taking out the trash is Herculean labor.

> They can always afford a smile and a friendly wave.

Still, everyone from the poorest pig farmer to the wealthiest merchant was always willing to lend a hand. There is an old Spanish saying — "The rich help the rich and the poor help those poorer than themselves." If a fruit seller runs out of fruit, you can bet that another fruit seller will lend him some. I remember once when we hitched a ride with a friend in his jam-packed truck. There must have been seven people in the car, with all of their luggage. Then we spotted three women hitchhiking. I thought there was no way that they could fit in the vehicle. Our friend, however, told them to get in the back of the truck, where they fit easily. I felt ashamed because I knew if I had been driving the truck, they would have been on that road a lot longer.

I discovered that just because you're not rich doesn't mean you can't have fun. When you don't have toys, a stick can be a sword, a cornhusk can become a doll, or a tree a jungle gym. Who needs a Nintendo when there are streams to splash in, rocks to scale and brothers to wrestle with? What those children experience is like nothing that can come from a remote control or video game. I remember playing on the edge of a lake in Bariloche, Argentina with some other kids, picking up rocks to try to find the ones with the most mica and trying to skip stones in the water. The strangest thing was that they didn't speak a word of English and I didn't speak any Spanish. Before that day, I couldn't imagine playing with another kid who I couldn't talk to.

> A stick can be a sword, a cornhusk can become a doll, or a tree a jungle gym.

However, the most incredible thing is how content everyone is. Waving at a complete stranger may seem strange where we live, but around the world it's no big deal. Smiles are passed around more quickly than can be returned, and street sellers will often chat so loudly to each other, you have to tap one on their shoulder to get their attention. I remember one frenzied night in Bangkok, when we were in a tuk-tuk (a cross between a bike and a rickshaw) and our driver was yelling good-naturedly to some of his friends on tuk-tuks across the street. Occasionally, they would toss packs of cigarettes to each other. At the time, I was almost scared to death and furious at our driver, but now I realize that those men drove their tuk-tuks day and night; they deserved to be able to have a little fun.

I'm usually not very big on morals. I find them too gushy and mushy, like "Every cloud has a silver lining." I think anyone who says that sounds like a weather forecaster, not an optimist.

However, this one I think is really good: You don't have to be rich or famous, or pretty (even though sometimes it might feel that way) to be happy. Traveling has sort of made me grow up, in a weird way. It hasn't made me bigger or stronger, but more aware. It's allowed me to open my eyes to the rest of the world. So next time I catch myself complaining about eating my Brussels sprouts, I'll remind myself to be grateful for what I have and keep my mouth shut.

— Chloe Rosenberg —
Chicken Soup for the Soul: Teens Talk Middle School

Learning to Love My Messy Life

Call it a clan, call it a network, call it a tribe, call it a family. Whatever you call it, whoever you are, you need one.
~Jane Howard

I slowly open my front door, praying I'll find some sort of normalcy when I enter. No such luck. Two children fly past me, my sister chasing after our brother, screaming for her doll back. There is pasta sauce splattered on our kitchen wall—artwork, my dad calls it. And my mom has set up shop smack in the middle, ironing a mountain of clothes while *Law and Order* blares from our television.

"I have five siblings," I mutter to my new neighbor, Michelle. "Sorry for the mess."

I whisk her away to my bedroom. It's really a room shared with my two sisters, but that was nothing a good bribe couldn't fix. They were "gone for the day" as Michelle and I flipped through magazines and painted our toenails. Mercifully, none of my brothers came barging in, and the smell of acetone was enough to keep my dad away. When it was time for dinner, Michelle skipped back to her house, telling me she'd call tomorrow.

She did, and I happily accepted her invitation to go to her house. Any place would be better than my house. Soon, I was standing at her front door, ringing the bell. A strange woman answered.

"Hello, Miss Suzanne," she said in broken English. "Michelle is upstairs."

That couldn't be her mother. I looked up at a gleaming white marble double staircase. Michelle appeared at the top, a huge smile on her face, motioning for me to follow her. I wanted to thank the woman who had opened the door, but she had disappeared.

To say Michelle's bedroom was huge is an understatement. It was more like a hotel suite, complete with king size bed, a sparkling chandelier and every toy imaginable. I had never seen anything so glamorous. She explained to me that the woman downstairs was her nanny, Marion. I wondered if Marion was going to hang out with us, but it quickly became clear that we had total freedom. The only interruption that day was Aura, the housekeeper, who was putting away freshly folded laundry. A nanny and a housekeeper at her disposal? Michelle was living the life.

I went over to Michelle's almost every day that summer, playing with her insane toy collection, unknowingly becoming more and more like family to her. I loved being in her immaculately clean home, having our lunches prepared for us like we were royalty. No chores, no siblings to annoy us, no parents to constantly nag us. I never noticed that her own parents were rarely home, and her nanny and housekeeper ignored her.

> I never noticed that her own parents were rarely home.

On one of those days, Michelle called me over earlier than usual. Her dad had given her something amazing called an Xbox, and she was dying to play it.

I raced over, flung open the door and announced my arrival. Aura crept up from the basement, greeting me the way she and Marion always did.

"Hello, Miss Suzanne. Michelle is upstairs."

"Thanks, Aura!" My voice echoed in her empty house.

It dawned on me. As I bounded up that glorious staircase, I thought, what did Michelle do when I wasn't there?

Sure, she had an endless supply of the latest gadgets. Sure, she had dance classes to go to. Sure, she had a nanny and a housekeeper. But who did she talk to? Who did she laugh with?

We spent all afternoon playing that Xbox. Time slipped away from us, and before we knew it, my mom was calling to tell me it was time for dinner. I looked over at Michelle, rolling my eyes as I begged my mom to let me miss dinner. This was not a battle I was going to win.

"Fine, Mom, I'll be home in five minutes," I grumbled

through my teeth. But before I could slam the phone down, an idea popped into my head.

"Wait, Mom!" I said. "Can Michelle have dinner with us tonight?"

We had to squeeze in an extra chair for her, but she didn't mind. Her eyes shined as she looked around at our table, talking excitedly with my sisters, shoveling food into her mouth like she hadn't eaten in days. She laughed at all the things that embarrassed me. She laughed at my dad's cluelessness. She laughed at my brothers flinging lettuce at each other. She even laughed when my sister tripped over our oven door, which had a broken latch that made it fall open every five minutes. Another thing to fix on our list of things to fix.

> Her eyes shined as she looked around at our table, talking excitedly with my sisters.

When our meal was finished, and all the dishes had been washed (assembly line style, the custom in our house), she turned to me and whispered, "You're so lucky you have such a big family. Can I have dinner with you all tomorrow night?"

I looked over at my sloppy siblings; my brothers were making a fort with our couch cushions, knocking over everything to make room for it, and my sisters were jumping up and down in the other room, dancing to a boombox that skipped whenever they hit the floor too hard. My parents were making espresso that bubbled over every time, adding yet another layer to the permanent coffee stain on our stove. Suddenly, my house — my crowded, messy, loud house — seemed like paradise.

— Suzanne De Vita —
Chicken Soup for the Soul: Think Positive for Kids

Is That All?

Gratitude is the best attitude.
~Author Unknown

Christmas was always an amazing time in my home when I was growing up. My parents didn't have a lot of money but they were always incredibly generous when it came to giving us presents. In fact, they didn't just give presents to us children. Every year they held a Christmas Eve party and gave all the kids in the neighborhood presents as well.

One year, when I was eight years old, I was hoping against hope that I would get a bike for Christmas. I made it clear in every way I knew how to my parents. I left hints all over the place.

On Christmas morning, we had our normal over-abundance of presents. All of us kids received present after present, with the last present being the "big" one. When we got to the apparent end of the presents I was very upset. My last present had not been the "big" one I had hoped for. There was no bike for me. I blurted out, "Is that all?" The moment I said it I knew

I had made a big mistake. That comment would have been inappropriate in any situation but after all those presents it was completely wrong-headed.

My parents looked unhappy, as my disappointment was obvious. I was so upset I didn't even realize how ungrate-

I didn't even realize how ungrateful I sounded.

ful I sounded. My entire family felt extremely uncomfortable and was on edge. For a few moments there was nothing but silence around the tree. I started to realize what an idiotic thing I had said. After my parents worked so hard, how could I complain that I did not receive a bike when I had received so many other things?

My parents continued to look very upset, and then something happened that made me feel even worse. My father got up and went outside the living room to the hallway. He came back wheeling the bicycle that they had been planning to give me after all the other presents were distributed.

Now I felt even worse than before — I had gotten the bike but had demonstrated for my parents and my siblings what an ungrateful person I actually was. How could I ever enjoy it after that? I did learn to enjoy my new bike, but it was never as good as it would have been if I hadn't said that stupid thing.

My parents were very wise people and they knew how to handle this. They told me to think about how I felt at the moment I saw that I had actually received the bike. They told me to remember that feeling so that I would never repeat that mistake and feel that way again.

For years after that, at the end of all the present giving, my father would ask me what I had to say to everyone. It had become a family joke. I would always say, "Is that all?" But what I really meant was "Thanks so much." And everyone knew that.

— Bill Rouhana —
Chicken Soup for the Soul: Think Positive for Kids

Feeding the Soul

Act as if what you do makes
a difference. It does.
-William James

White puffs of bread lined up in front of me, with seas of mayonnaise spread over them. How many times had I done this? How many more times would I be forced to do it?

The pink circles of meat and perfectly square blocks of cheese made slapping sounds as I threw them down. My dad would soon be leaving to feed the homeless.

> My father and several volunteers from the church gathered every day in the park to feed the hungry.

Every afternoon we went to the store, and the people there would give us things that were past the expiration date but hadn't gone bad. Usually we received things like sliced vegetables, pieces of fruit, bread, and slices of cake or pie. We gave these to the homeless along with the sandwiches and tea.

My father and several volunteers from the church gathered every day in the park to feed the hungry and teach anyone who was willing to listen about God.

Boy was I glad I didn't have to go to the feedings. It was enough trouble just getting everything ready. I really didn't understand why my father bothered with it. I couldn't wait for him to leave. I looked forward to a whole Saturday by myself. I planned to watch some television, talk with my friends on the phone, and maybe do some shopping during the afternoon.

It didn't take long for my plans to change and my happiness to dissolve. Dad came in while I was finishing and stood behind me.

"I'm going to need your help today. Some of the others that usually help me won't be able to make it."

"Dad, I can't today," I whined. "I have plans, television, friends, shopping, and I was maybe going to go to the pool."

He just gave me the you-should-be-ashamed-of-yourself look.

"Fine." I pouted. "It's not like I have a life."

"I really appreciate it. It will just be us today."

He left the room.

That's probably because everyone else finally realized that it's all just a waste of time, I thought to myself. You're not really helping anybody.

I was really upset my day was now ruined.

I finished packing the sandwiches and followed Dad out to the van. I wanted to cry. This was going to be the worst day ever. My dad always drove the church van, which also contained clothes and small bags filled with personal items such as combs, toothbrushes, toothpaste, razors, and deodorant.

He pulled out of the driveway to head downtown. I looked out the window and watched as we drove past kids playing in their front yards. I felt like a prisoner forced to perform community service.

When we arrived at the park, people were already gathered under a tree waiting for us. We opened the back of the van and pulled out a long cafeteria table and some chairs. I put the table on one side of the van with the food on it, while my dad lined up chairs on the other side for them to sit in.

In between the table and the people was a single chair for my dad to sit in. I watched as he opened his guitar case. He smiled at me and turned to his congregation to play, sing songs of praise, and read from the Bible.

I couldn't believe how many people were there, and all of them homeless. I was surprised to learn my dad knew most of them by name. He also seemed to know what each one needed and what they had suffered through that landed them on the street.

One man told me if it hadn't been for my father he didn't think he would have found Jesus.

"Even when the weather is bad and the shelter has closed its door to us, your dad is still here. It's the one thing folks like us can count on, and we don't soon forget his kindness."

After the sermon we put what food we had left into bags and handed them out. That's when I noticed a man still sitting in a chair. He had a badly swollen, purple face.

My father noticed my stare and explained a member of a gang had found the man sleeping in the street and thought it would be fun to throw bricks at him.

While my father went to talk with him about the Lord, I climbed into the back of the van and started handing out some articles of clothing.

A girl about my age came up to me from across the street. Her face was stained with dirt and her dark hair was a mass of stringy curls. I noticed right away that she was barefoot.

"Do you have some shoes, about a size six?" she asked meekly.

I stared into her blue eyes for a moment, unable to believe someone so similar to me could live like this. I had never thought about the possibility of homeless children.

She didn't look me in the eye for very long and I was worried I had made her uncomfortable.

I looked back into the van and saw only one pair of shoes left. Please let them be a six, I thought. I picked them up and turned them over. Exactly a six.

> I realized I should have been thankful for everything I have.

"Thank you!" she cried happily. She slid them on and ran back across the street. I felt all warm inside as I watched her leave.

When everyone was gone, we loaded things back into the van. Now I understood why my father did so much to help the homeless. I could tell he loved seeing their smiles of happiness. I did too.

I was so worried that morning about missing out on my fun day. I realized I should have been thankful for everything I have. That day with my dad taught me that there will always be someone smarter, prettier, or richer than me, and there will also always be someone less fortunate. The difference is in the individual willing to take the opportunity to help others, even if it means sacrificing something of their own.

— Sylvia Ney —
Chicken Soup for the Soul: Just for Preteens

Against All Odds

Turn your wounds into wisdom.
-Oprah Winfrey

I faced the struggle of conquering the difficult preteen years of my life without a mother to guide me. My mom died very suddenly when I was eight years old, leaving me, my dad, and my twelve-year-old sister without the glue that had held our lives together. Although this tragedy was very difficult for me because I was so young, I can't imagine what my sister must have felt, losing her mother at such a crucial time in her life. And, a few years later, it was my turn to experience the pain of crossing the threshold into my teenage years without the invaluable guidance of my mom.

> I wished I could shake them and tell them how lucky they were to have a mom.

Many days, I would listen to my friends at school complain about what, to me, seemed to be such petty problems. It was different for me. Often, I would lend an ear as they vented about various issues, including how much they hated their parents or their mothers. Deep down, I wished I could shake them and tell them how lucky they were to have a mom, even if they didn't always get along. I would have given anything to have my mom there to give me advice about "girl things" during that time — I would even have gladly welcomed the occasional argument or disagreement, just to have her around. Sometimes, I wanted to tell my friends that their problems were nothing — try getting your first period or going shopping for your first bra without your mom there to help you. I felt lost, to say the least.

Don't get me wrong — my dad did a wonderful job of raising my sister and me on his own, and I was lucky to have an older sister to turn to who could give me advice. But it just wasn't the same. Everyone knows that nothing can replace the presence of a girl's mother in her life — and the loss leaves a void that can never truly be filled, by anyone or anything.

I remember one particularly difficult day at school, when a peer in my Spanish class made a joke having to do with my mom, apparently not knowing that she had passed away. I ran to the bathroom, locked myself in one of the stalls and cried. On another occasion, I was online and received a message from someone with a very hurtful user name having to do with my mom. It even had my name in it, so I knew this was an intentional attack on me by somebody who knew me — not an innocent joke made by someone who didn't know better — and I was heartbroken at how hurtful people could be. I didn't want to go to school the next day because I was so upset and had no way of knowing who had played this cruel joke on me. I was afraid I might end up having a conversation with this person and not even know it, or that people might be making fun of me behind my back.

I always felt that having lost my mom made me different from everyone else — that it would always brand me as being an outsider, the girl without a mom. I often wondered if it occurred to my schoolmates when I passed by — "There goes the motherless girl...." Some days, I would have given anything to just wake up with a pimple or have worn an ugly outfit — those seemed like such simpler problems. Most days, I felt very much alone.

> I realized at a fairly young age just how strong and independent I was.

Despite the challenges of navigating the trials of life as a preteen girl without a mother, I learned a lot about myself from this experience. I realized at a fairly young age just how strong and independent I was, and how much I was really capable of. While I knew that nothing could ever ease the hurt of being forced to live these years of my life without my mom by my side, I realized eventually that I would be okay one way or another. My dad always told us that we had already been through the hardest thing two young girls could ever be faced with, and if we could get through that, we could do anything. At some point, I finally began to realize that he was right and adopted this attitude myself.

Life makes no guarantees — not to any of us. The only thing within our control is how we choose to handle the obstacles life places before us, whatever they may be. The thing to remember is, with the right attitude, you will never meet an obstacle that is insurmountable. No matter what happens today, there will still be tomorrow — and you will make it through. I'm living proof.

—Julia K. Agresto—
Chicken Soup for the Soul: Just for Preteens

The Shirt Off My Back

**If you haven't any charity in your heart,
you have the worst kind of heart trouble.
~Bob Hope**

t was as if a supernatural force had overtaken me. My heart fluttered and my legs had a mind of their own.

"Look, Mom!" I exclaimed, pointing to a giant sign across the mall.

"What is it?" she asked.

"Everything is ninety percent off!" My voice reached an octave higher than normal.

"Let's take a look," Mom said.

"Wow! Good find, Andrea," said my sister Juliana.

We marched straight to our favorite store. Once inside, we found ourselves amidst the bustling frenzy of shoppers. We strolled through the cloud of perfume, past the cosmetic counters, directly to the racks of clothes.

"These T-shirts are only two dollars!" Juliana exclaimed.

We snaked through the crowd. I started grabbing as many shirts as I could. There were five different shades of purple and since I couldn't decide, I took all of them.

"This sale is awesome!" I said as I flipped through the sea of blues.

"Try them on," Mom said. "They are so cheap."

I snatched them all off the hangers. Before I went into the changing room, Mom whipped out her calculator, punched in numbers and calculated our savings.

I started grabbing as many shirts as I could.

"These jeans are only seven dollars," Juliana said, leaning over Mom's shoulder.

Even though I didn't need them, I carried the jeans into the fitting room. The shopping ritual was something I experienced each year during the holidays and before school. I had taken whatever was in reach and the miniscule changing room was overflowing with clothes. As I stood knee-deep in a colorful mountain of T-shirts, I realized I did not have enough room to store them all. Did I really need these?

I started thinking about all the children who never got new clothes. I lived the first year of my life in an orphanage in Buzau, Romania where the children had nothing. My sister and I were both adopted from there, and my mother made sure to ship boxes of clothes to the orphans in Romania every year. Each summer, my parents, sister and I dedicated a day to sifting through our closets and choosing some clothing to share.

Sometimes my mother convinced me to give away clothing that I still liked a lot, but other times it wasn't as hard as I often had brand new clothing that I had been given for Christmas or birthdays that I didn't even use.

Did I really need these?

As I stood among the piles of clothes in the cramped dressing room, I turned to Mom as she neatly folded the shirts I set aside to purchase. "I have enough," I said.

Mom stared blankly.

"I'm not going to buy these."

"Which ones did you decide not to buy?"

"I want all of them, but I don't need anything." I licked my lips and sighed deeply. "I'm not going to buy any of these." My eyes glistened with tears as I pictured dozens of kids running around, playing happily in my hand-me-down clothes. I certainly didn't need any new clothing, when I already has so much. A smile tugged at the corners of my mouth. "I need to go home and clean out my closet." I don't know any of the Romanian orphans, but I know I would give them the shirt off my back.

— Andrea Canale —
Chicken Soup for the Soul: Think Positive for Kids

Chapter 7

TREASURE YOUR FAMILY

Just Do It

*No one is useless in this world who
lightens the burdens of another.*
~Charles Dickens

As a preteen, I was pretty lazy when it came to "doing" for my family. I worked hard at school, did tons of homework, practiced for piano lessons, and sometimes babysat my younger sister. Still, I found myself regularly resisting the urge to help out at home with even the simplest things.

If my mother or father asked me to do something, I would do it: not a problem. But the fact that I always needed to be asked or told to do things — things I could plainly see needed doing — undoubtedly bugged my parents. What Mom and Dad didn't realize, though, was that by age ten my resistance to chipping in even bugged me!

For a long time, I wasn't bothered enough to actually do anything about it. But my guilty conscience — knowing I could and should do more for my folks, and not just when asked — led me to feel pretty bad about myself.

Every Wednesday afternoon, for example, my mother drove me to another town for a piano lesson. During my half-hour lesson, she'd rush to the nearby grocery store and buy a week's worth of groceries. Given the fact that my mom had just driven me twelve miles there, twelve miles back, paid for my lesson, and bought me a candy bar, you'd think I'd be grateful and gracious enough to help her bring the groceries into the house without being asked. But I wasn't.

> You'd think I'd be grateful and gracious enough to help her bring the groceries into the house.

I knew I should help her. But with homework weighing heavily on my mind—and with "me" still the center of my universe—I generally just brought in an armload and left the rest for Mom as I ran to my room, shut the door, and started studying.

Don't get me wrong: being conscientious about school is a good thing, and I know my parents appreciated my hard work and good grades. But the thing is, even holed up in my room, I still felt guilty about not helping my mother more. Sure, I had work to do—but she'd worked all day, too! And after hauling in those bags, and putting the food away, Mom still had to whip up a tasty dinner for the five of us. Small wonder I felt guilty.

A similar situation occurred on summer weekends as my family headed north to our rustic lakeside cabin. Each of us kids was expected to pack our own basket of clothes and toys, carry it to the car and, later, bring it inside the camp. But besides our individual baskets, that station wagon was always jam-packed with coolers, camp gear, and bags of food. Once again — if asked — I'd help carry in everything else. But if left to my own devices, I was much more apt to dump my basket inside, then head outdoors to explore the woods. Exploring trumped helping every time.

Exploring is a good thing, sure, and it turned me into a lifelong naturalist. But my "not helping" was gradually becoming a bigger and bigger problem for me because in my heart and my head I knew I was skirting responsibility — not to mention, it obviously made my parents cranky to have to continually ask for my help.

In my heart and my head I knew I was skirting responsibility.

Deep down I wanted to change my ways. But I also realized that once I did change, there'd be no going back. Once I took on more responsibilities, my parents would start expecting more of me. At age ten, I sensed that this one small change would mark the start of something far bigger: my personal transition from a cared-for, semi-spoiled child to a more mature, responsible, caring and giving young person.

I'll never forget the Wednesday I made a conscious decision to jump in and see what happened. Returning home from my lesson, I disappeared into my room, as usual. But once inside, I felt that deep and burning shame. Dumping my schoolbooks and music on the bed, I abruptly opened my door and headed back to the garage to help my mother.

I'm sure Mom thanked me that day, but her thanks are not what I remember. What I remember most is the incredible sense of peace and satisfaction I felt after helping her. Working hard at school always made me feel good. But what surprised me that day was how happy I felt just helping my mom — all on my own.

At the time, I imagine Mom wondered: "Is this a one-time deal or will Wendy help me again next week?"

Unknown to her, I'd already vowed to pitch in every single Wednesday — and from that day on, I did. It was such a small action. Yet what a nice little difference it made in my mom's life! And what a huge difference it made in mine. The selfishness and guilt I'd struggled with for so long suddenly vanished, replaced by a warm glow of pride.

As for those summer treks to the lake, ditto! Instead of just carrying my own stuff, I began returning to the car for more loads — even when my father was in a really grouchy "long week at work" mood. The first time I did it, Dad probably wondered the same thing as Mom: "Is this a one-time deal?"

But over time, I showed my sincerity by continuing to help out with the loading and unloading. The neat thing was, the more I helped out, the better I felt about myself and my place within my family. As Mom and Dad realized they could count on me more, our trips became far less stressful, too. In short, it was a win-win situation for everyone.

Sometimes the little things we put off doing the longest turn out to be the simplest things to accomplish. Helping out more — and offering to help rather than waiting to be asked — made my parents and me a lot happier. And feeling happy trumps feeling guilty any day.

— Wendy Hobday Haugh —
Chicken Soup for the Soul: Think Positive for Kids

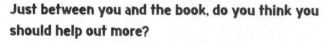

Wendy figured out how to help at home and it made her feel good.

Just between you and the book, do you think you should help out more?

Circle one: **Yes   No**

List three new ways you can help out at home:

1. _____

2. _____

3. _____

Jonny and Me

When you look at your life, the greatest happinesses are family happinesses.
~Joyce Brothers

My family sometimes talks about "Before Jonny" and "After Jonny." But I've never known life without my special brother.

Not that we're not all special — at least that's what my parents say. We are fifty-four weeks apart, which to some people means we're "Irish Twins." And in a way, we really were like twins when we were little.

Now we're pretty different. That's because Jonny has Down syndrome, or as my mom calls it, "A Little Extra" — an extra chromosome on his twenty-first pair. I finally understood this when we made DNA models with gumdrops and pretzel sticks at school.

Jonny isn't really all that different, but his differences are enough to make him stand out in a crowd. Over the years, I've seen a lot of different reactions from people in all sorts of situations. But while I've heard stories about kids giving disabled kids a rough time, I've never seen that in the places where we've lived. In fact, Jonny seems to bring out the best in the people he meets. Now, when he walks down the halls of our high school, he's greeted with tons of high fives and cries of "Hey, Jonny!"

Jonny seems to bring out the best in the people he meets.

For a while, in middle school, I even worried that Jonny was more popular than me. When I told my dad how I felt, he said that Jonny had a long road ahead of him — and that he needed all the confidence he could get in his early years. Someday, my dad said, those people high-fiving and "Hey Jonny-ing" him would be the same people who might give jobs to him and other people with disabilities. My dad told me that soon middle school would be over. He said that what I was feeling was normal for a girl with an older brother in the same school and, as he often liked to repeat, "This too shall pass." I used to hate it when my dad said that, but as I get older I start to see that he has a point.

And it did pass — my mixed feelings about Jonny's popularity. Now I'm happy for him. I'm happy we live in a town where he can have a lot of friends and I'm proud of our school where four years ago a senior girl with Down syndrome was voted Homecoming Queen.

While my mom and dad have had to work hard to help Jonny reach his potential, they've worked as hard to help me reach mine. Jonny and I share a love of Broadway musicals and both of us hope someday to work onstage.

Seeing Jonny's life unfold has helped me see that there's a plan for mine as well. Just like Jonny's Down syndrome, our love of music and acting are things that were present in us the day we were born.

> **Four years ago a senior girl with Down syndrome was voted Homecoming Queen.**

My parents say having a baby is like getting a gift from God. As they grow up, that gift is slowly unwrapped until we see what's inside.

Jonny's little extra was obvious the minute he was born. Unwrapping my package may have taken a little longer, but if there's one thing Jonny has taught our family, it's that each of us is a little different. But what's most important are the ways in which we are the same.

— Madeleine Curtis —
Chicken Soup for the Soul: Teens Talk Middle School

Sibling Rivalry

Siblings—the definition that comprises
love, strife, competition
and forever friends.
~Byron Pulsifer

The day my parents brought me home from the hospital, my sister Patty started a rivalry between the two of us. As I slept she reached into the crib, grabbed the baby bottle and said, "My ba-ba."

The fight began at that moment and continued for many years. I weighed just under six pounds at birth and remained smaller than my sister for most of our growing up years. Bigger, tougher and far more aggressive than I, she artfully directed my actions like an Army staff sergeant. I dutifully obeyed her mostly from fear of retaliation, but as I grew, I developed my own personal methods of payback.

Mom worked long hours and during my elementary school years I got out of school before my sister. I walked home, usually to an empty place. One of the entrances to the kitchen was in the hallway. After a particularly difficult day, I waited patiently the whole afternoon. Just before she arrived, I hid beside the refrigerator and out of sight from anyone coming down the hall. Holding my breath and keeping completely still and quiet, I paused until a split second after she passed and then jumped behind her, grabbed her shoulder and said, "Boo!" She always jumped. Sometimes she hit me, but realized quickly that I'd get her back later if she did.

Patty had a strong fear of someone kidnapping her. The thought of a black-gloved man grabbing her from behind terrified her. On some occasions after we fought, she sat down to practice piano. One day, as she became more engrossed in notes, scales and her most recent songs, I tiptoed to Mom's bedroom and retrieved black leather gloves from the dresser drawer. I slipped them on my small hands, pushed the lock in on the bathroom door (leaving it opened of course) and returned to the living room with great stealth. At the peak of her practice time, I approached her back and threw my hands over her eyes. Her blood-curdling scream raced through the house as I jumped back in a fit of giggles, avoiding her fists. Before she recovered and stumbled from the piano bench, I ran to the bathroom and slammed the door behind me. What followed was a loud mixture of my cackling and her pounding fists on the door, but I stayed behind the locked door until I heard the piano again.

Eventually, I grew tired of the sibling rivalry. I really detested fighting with my sister. My fifth grade year arrived with turmoil at home and our parents' divorce. More than ever, I needed a big sister's love instead of an enemy. One day, I was helping the school counselor check some standardized tests, and we began to talk. She knew my family well.

I asked, "Why does my sister always pick fights with me?"

With a world of wisdom, she didn't answer my question. Instead, in a gentle voice, she said, "You know, it will hurt her more if you don't fight back. Try to just ignore it when she wants to argue."

> I needed a big sister's love instead of an enemy.

The next time we started fighting, the counselor's words flitted around my mind. Why not try it? A little uncertain, but willing to try, I ignored Patty. She kept pushing. To make sure she got the point, I took it to the next level.

I said, "It's so quiet here by myself."

She muttered something insulting.

I retorted, "I hate being all alone in this big ole house." I made sure she got the point that I was ignoring her.

We kept going back and forth for a while, but I never broke down. Sometimes I kept silent and at other times spoke only to myself. I directed nothing I said to her.

In sheer frustration, she begged, "You can hit me! Please just talk to me."

What do you know? It worked.

We repeated this process many more times until one day the fighting stopped. We began a friendship, and over the next two years became best friends. Although we still had occasional fights and sometimes intensely disliked each other, it no longer felt like a daily battle between us. We watched out for each other and shared secrets. Sometimes we spent hours telling each other our dreams. We passed the phone to each

We watched out for each other and shared secrets.

other when our grandmother called and talked for hours. We covered each other when someone cracked a glass table during a forbidden indoor game of blind man's bluff. Neither of us knew how in the world that table got broken, and neither admitted that we invited neighborhood kids inside that day. I removed her glasses at night when she fell asleep reading.

By the time we made it to junior high school, we genuinely liked each other.

I had a job working in the library during one of my class periods. One day, her English class came into the room. As I checked out her book, one of her classmates was shocked by the revelation that we were sisters. "You can't be sisters," they said. "You like each other too much." We both smiled.

Throughout the years, we watched most of our friends who had sisters fight like cats and dogs. Instead, I treasured my sister, who doubled as a best friend during some difficult years of my young life. The baby bottle incident became a family joke, and I learned that a sister could be a great friend.

She still is.

— Lisa Bell —
Chicken Soup for the Soul: Just for Preteens

Where I Belong

We should not be asking who this child
belongs to, but who belongs to this child.
—Jim Gritter

"Why didn't your parents want you? How does that make you feel?" "Is your real family dead?" "Will you have to go back someday?"

It wasn't easy being adopted — especially being a brown girl from Central America, with two white parents. Until seventh grade, it hadn't been too much of an issue for me. I'd gone to a small church school with the same people I pretty much saw seven days a week. We all knew each other as well as if we were related, and we'd grown up together from babyhood. Everyone knew I was adopted, and it was no big deal.

> It wasn't easy being adopted—especially being a brown girl from Central America, with two white parents.

But when I was twelve, I left my safe cocoon for a bigger, public middle school. Like my elementary school, the new school was mostly white. I was used to that. What I wasn't used to were all the questions.

Now, I know — from the statistics — that there were probably as many as three or four other adopted kids in my class. But they were the same color as their parents, so nobody had to know their private business. I, on the other hand, couldn't hide.

It wasn't so bad when my mom came alone to help out at school or attend a meeting. When kids saw her, they just assumed I had a Latino dad. There were other mixed-race students in my class and, just like I'd grown up with the same group of kids at my elementary school, these kids had all grown up together, too. They were used to mixed marriages.

At first, I didn't want anybody to know. I just hoped and prayed only one parent would show up to things. Then, for all anyone knew, I could just be another biracial kid. But, all too soon, people found out, and I had to start answering questions.

Of course, a lot of people didn't care either way. But when you're twelve and you feel very different, it really seems like everybody is staring and whispering — when in actuality, they aren't even paying any attention to you at all.

Some kids were just innocently curious. Others were downright mean about it. They were the kind of kids that tell their younger brother or sister, "You're adopted" — like it's a bad thing — even when they aren't.

At first, it felt as if I was defending myself. Maybe it was none of their business, but brushing them off would only have made things worse. I had to admit I was adopted. I had to explain why I was adopted, and what that meant.

It was frustrating a lot of the time. People just didn't get it. They couldn't understand why somebody wouldn't be living with their "real" parents. They couldn't imagine what it would be like, living with "strangers."

It drove me crazy. What did "real" mean, anyway? My adoptive parents were as real as anybody else's. I was their "real" kid. We sure weren't artificial. And after twelve years together, we were anything but strangers.

As time went by, I made true friends. They came over to our house and hung out. My mom or dad drove us to the mall or the movies. My friends were soon as comfortable with my family as the kids I'd grown up with.

But some of the other kids still didn't get it. It was as if they thought adoption was wrong or scary. I guess I could have kept trying to get through to them, but finally I realized they would probably never understand — and that was not my problem.

> **Adopted kids are just like any other kids.**

Adopted kids are just like any other kids. When we get in trouble, we get grounded. Our parents clean up our messes and stay with us when we're sick. They yell at us when they get mad. They're proud when we do well. Sometimes, they hurt our feelings or don't understand us, or they let us down. And sometimes they stand up for us, or they sit and listen when we are sad or worried. Adoptive families are forever, and we are just like anyone else.

It wasn't till I got a little older that I realized how lucky

I really was, and that adoption was something that made our family even more special. I had friends with parents who were in jail or had just disappeared. One girl lived in a group foster home. Some kids were failing out or school or doing drugs, and their parents didn't even seem to care.

I am blessed to have a home and a family that cares about me. I know, too, that I'm blessed to have a birth family that loved me enough to let me be adopted when they weren't able to provide for me. A lot of people aren't so lucky. I am where I belong.

— Marcela Dario Fuentes —
Chicken Soup for the Soul: Just for Preteens

The Magic

In every walk with nature, one receives
far more than he seeks.
~John Muir

I t was that special time of the evening when my grandmother and I took our nightly walk to the harbor. I
grabbed my flip-flops and sweater, waiting patiently at
the front door for Gram to come. My favorite time of
day was about to start.

Off we went, starting down the winding path through
the woods, hand in hand. As we walked, Gram pointed out
the treasures that the woods held—a
cluster of lady's slippers reaching out
of the earth; an old, gnarled apple
tree filled with fruit; a tiny chipmunk
scampering across the path; and birds,
so many beautiful birds, each with its
own special call.

> My favorite
> time of day
> was about
> to start.

Gram took these things we saw and created a story for me,
one that was different each night. The lady's slippers might be

parasols or balloons for the fairies who dwelled in the forest. The old, gnarled apple tree might be a secret hiding place where gnomes lived. The scampering chipmunk might be a royal ride for a princess, and the beautiful birds were guardians of the forest, magical creatures who cared for all the animals who made the woods their home.

The setting sun shimmered through the tree branches, dappling the ground in front of us, as our nightly adventure continued. Gram shared her secrets about all that we saw as we

"There is magic everywhere. Always look for the magic."

walked along. The path opened up in front of us to reveal a clearing that overlooked a shining harbor. Gram said mermaids lived there, taking care of the seas and the boats that were anchored there.

As we walked along, enjoying our time together, Gram told me how lucky we were to be surrounded by the magnificence of the world around us. "There is magic everywhere. Always look for the magic."

As the years went on, Gram and I continued our walks, sharing in the beauty that we experienced together. It became woven into the fabric of our lives, into the very way we perceived life and its many gifts. It was central to our relationship and created a special bond between us.

The time came when Gram could no longer go on our walks. I would bring our walks to her, reading stories and poems that captured the essence of the world around us, the beauty of nature, and the memories we shared together. When I finished reading, Gram would always say, "Always look for the magic." That phrase had become a powerful constant between us, one that epitomized all the love and adventures we shared.

Gram passed away surrounded by family and loved ones. As I was leaving her side, ready to steel myself for the grief and longing that would settle in, my cousin came to me with a small, foil-wrapped package tied lovingly with gold ribbon. My name was written on the top. Gram had given her strict instructions about the handful of treasures she was to put inside — acorns, small stones, colorful leaves, and a small conch shell, like the ones we had seen so many times at the harbor. A small piece of folded paper was also inside. I opened it tearfully and read the words, "Always look for the magic." At that moment, I knew I had not really lost Gram. She would be with me always, in the magic she had taught me about, in the simple beauty that surrounded us. I would look for the magic... always.

— MJ Keenan —
Chicken Soup for the Soul: Grandparents

The Family Portrait

You don't choose your family. They are
God's gift to you, as you are to them.
—Desmond Tutu

In my father's house, in my old bedroom, is a dresser. The dresser belonged to my older sister before she moved away. Then I inherited it. The smooth brown surface is free of scratches and marks. All the handles and knobs are still attached. It looks brand new, but this deceptive piece of furniture has been the silent guardian of my most precious treasure for twelve years.

Hidden behind the dresser and covered in more than a decade of dust is a family portrait of my mother and father, my older sister and brother, and me. It's a reminder of life before my parents divorced, when the five of us equaled a family.

I don't have to brush away the dust to see that I am the only one really smiling in the picture. A precocious toddler, I may have been the only one who didn't know at the time that my family was falling apart.

When I was four years old, my parents divorced. I didn't

understand what that meant. All that my innocent mind understood was that mother didn't live with us anymore. The portrait remained on the living room wall and to me that signified that I still had a family. A few years later, to my dismay, my sister pulled the portrait down.

I spent the next several years struggling with the divorce. Our home became less and less like a "normal" home and I became envious of my friends who still had a mother and father who lived together. I sought the approval of my friends' parents, hoping to be adopted into their loving clans. I longed for family meals and family vacations. I wanted someone to rub my back when I wasn't feeling well.

> When I was four years old, my parents divorced.

My parents started dating other people and with each new woman my father brought home I felt utterly and hopelessly lost. Deep down inside I believed that my parents really did love each other and would get back together someday. I struggled to define what a family is. I felt like I was living with strangers because everyone was off doing their own thing and I was left alone. Home became a cold place where I didn't want to be.

I don't know where the portrait was stored, but when I was in seventh grade, my dad remarried and we moved into my stepmother's house. While unpacking boxes, I found it and quickly hid it behind the dresser. It was my treasure — my reminder of a time when I had a complete family. I was afraid if my stepmother found it she would throw it away and my family would be lost forever.

That first Thanksgiving in my new home was when I realized I had found exactly what I thought I had lost when my sister took the portrait down — a family. My stepmother cooked all day and the house was filled with mouth-watering smells of turkey, stuffing, biscuits and pumpkin pie. It was cold outside, but the house was warm and cozy. Seven of us gathered around the dining room table and our chattering voices filled the room. For the first time in a long time, I was happy.

> That first Thanksgiving in my new home was when I realized I had found exactly what I thought I had lost.

I realized that day that a family doesn't have to live under the same roof. Even though my parents are divorced, they're still my family. They still love me and I love them. The great thing about a family is how it can grow to include stepparents and stepsiblings. There never was another family portrait, but I don't need a picture to remind me what a family is.

— Valerie D. Benko —
Chicken Soup for the Soul: Just for Preteens

Tell Them You Love Them Now

> I love you and that's the beginning
> and end of everything.
> ~F. Scott Fitzgerald

As a preteen, I loved inspirational stories. I devoured *Reader's Digest* and *Guideposts*. I treasured any heart-warming tale that gave me something to think about and I tried to incorporate the lessons I learned into my life.

One memorable story was about a person whose parent died suddenly. The last words spoken between them had been words of anger. This was not an unfamiliar situation to someone my age. As we try to establish our individuality, we push back against the people with whom we feel safe, the people we know won't turn away.

But it had never occurred to me that my parents could die suddenly. My mother and I were close, but she was the rule keeper in our house, so we argued at times.

But it wasn't Mom I thought about; it was my dad. Dad was a drinker and not one to share his feelings other than the anger or humor he sometimes revealed when he was in a storytelling mood. I started to think about my dad and his life, and the emotional distance between him and his family. My dad went to work in the mines at age thirteen, after his much-loved dad was killed in a mining accident. He had grown up too fast and too hard.

I decided that every night, before I went to bed, I would tell my dad I loved him. He was not a hugger, so I decided that when I said, "I love you," I would kiss him on the top of his bald head.

> Every night, before I went to bed, I would tell my dad I loved him.

The first night I did this, he jerked his head away and looked at me like I was a crazy person. I was undeterred. Every night, it was "Good night Dad, I love you" and a kiss on his head. After a while, I noticed he stopped pulling away and began to lean in a bit. Encouraged by this, I began to add a small hug. He did not resist.

Then one night, weeks into the process, he said gruffly, "I love you, too." I paused for just a moment, struck by the wonder of it. I turned away quickly because I was not sure how Dad might respond to the tears spilling down my cheeks.

This changed how I saw my dad. He was not the scary guy who drank too much and had unpredictable flashes of anger. He was the guy sitting at the kitchen table every night with a beer in front of him, often with his head in his hands, who told me he loved me.

I began to sit with him on those nights he seemed talkative. As we shared a love of dogs, I got him to tell me stories about his favorite dogs, especially Mike, who followed Dad down to the mines every day. These stories revealed the tenderhearted side of my dad.

These stories revealed the tenderhearted side of my dad.

Many years later, after I was long married and living in another state, my father began to have some health problems. He refused to go to the doctor. My mother called and asked me to come home to "talk some sense into him; he'll listen to you."

I had already reserved my flight when she called to say, "Never mind, your father made a doctor's appointment." I decided to go home anyway and asked her not to tell Dad because I wanted to surprise him.

When he found me in the house, sitting at the kitchen table in "his spot," he was startled. In his usual brusque way, he blurted out, "What are you doing here?"

"Mom said you weren't feeling well, so I came home." He turned toward me and looked me straight in the eyes.

"Well, now I know I am loved." There was no hugging or overt emotion, just words from the heart.

Now he knows he is loved! I do not think he could have made such a vulnerable statement if we had not had those years of nightly "I love you's." After he turned and left the room, my mother expressed her amazement as well.

"Jude, you were right to come anyway. Your father needed you."

That doctor's appointment was the beginning of the end for my dad. He had fought off colon cancer more than twenty years before, but now was in a cancer fight that he couldn't win. Though he had surgery and we thought we had time left together, he died unexpectedly.

Fortunately, I knew what my final words to him were. I had stopped at the hospital on my way to the airport. I was returning to my home to check on my family, planning to bring them back with me to have time with Dad.

He was sound asleep. His nurse offered to wake him up, but I said "no." I wanted to carry with me this image of him sleeping so peacefully. So I just leaned in, kissed his warm head, rosy from the sponge bath she had just given him, and said, "I love you, Dad."

When I got to the funeral home and saw him in his casket, it didn't seem real. But when I leaned in and gave him a kiss on the top of his bald head to say one more "I love you," the coldness of his skin made it clear he was truly gone.

What was not gone is what I know: I am loved. I know he went to his grave knowing he was loved, too. And I'm eternally grateful to that long-ago author who wrote the story that got me to say it now, not to wait. I say "I love you" all the time — to my son and my beloved dogs, to my extended family and my friends. The beautiful thing is, most of them say it back. Often, like with my dad, they don't say it right away. But once we hit our stride, the rhythm is steady.

—Jude Walsh—
Chicken Soup for the Soul: The Best Advice I Ever Heard

Chapter 8

LOOK PAST THE OBVIOUS

Chicken Soup
for the Soul

The Bully and the Braid

Kindness is in our power,
even when fondness is not.
~Samuel Johnson

"Somebody's gonna get beat up," announced May Jordan while casually leaning against the monkey bars. Frozen by fear, the group of students surrounding May silently hoped that her latest victim wasn't among them, but they knew full well that there was always a chance. "We'll see after school," she said before flexing her large muscles for effect. Meanwhile, I hugged my Cabbage Patch Kid on a nearby bench, trying desperately to ignore the lump in my throat; it now felt the size of a small tangerine. I couldn't wait for recess to end.

I loved school, I really did. But since May had transferred in, Elliott Elementary had become an uncomfortable place. At approximately five feet eight inches, May was the tallest kid in our fifth grade class, and, in fact had already sprung well above every student in the school. Although her height was intimidating, it wasn't a problem — her attitude was. No part of the student population was beyond the reach of May's menacing taunts: She routinely hurled insults at innocent third graders who were too afraid to defend themselves; she blatantly bullied boys during gym class; she even threatened to snatch the patches off the sashes of Girl Scouts.

After carefully looking over their shoulders so as to ensure that May wasn't within earshot, many students contended that she was all bark and no bite. But I wasn't so sure. I had managed to fly under May's radar — and I wanted to keep it that way. But all that changed when I showed up for school one morning with a new (albeit unoriginal) hairstyle. Apparently, by wearing my hair in a French braid, I had managed to change my fate.

> I immediately came up with a plan, which involved hiding out in the bathroom at the end of the school day.

It all started when my best friend, Jaime, said my hair looked nice. I noticed May's piercing glare — and it made me uncomfortable — but I remained focused on my math worksheet. Then came May's daunting proclamation as she passed me in the cafeteria: "Nice braid. Somebody might cut it off."

I was scared. But what really sent me into a tailspin was when May, who was now clear across the room, moved her fingers to imitate a pair of scissors in motion. My stomach dropped to my knees, and I immediately came up with a plan, which involved hiding out in the bathroom at the end of the school day so as to avoid running into May on the walk home.

I awoke the next morning with a start and scurried to the bathroom to watch my mother get ready for work. Although my watching her had become routine, she knew something was up.

"What's wrong, Courtney?" my mother said, while sweeping the apples of her cheeks with blush.

"Nothing," I replied.

"You're lying. Tell me the truth," she persisted.

"May Jordan wants to cut off my braid," I sputtered with a mouth thick with saliva; tears began to fall.

"If she can see that you're not afraid, she will stop."

"She's a bully," my mother said earnestly while taking my chin in her hand. "She thrives on making others scared, that's all. Don't be afraid of her, Courtney. If she can see that you're not afraid, she will stop. I'll bet she's like everybody else — she just wants to fit in and make friends. Perhaps she just doesn't know how."

I rolled my mother's words around in my head. She did have a valid point. May wasn't so great at making friends. Maybe — just maybe — underneath all that toughness was a regular fifth grader who simply wanted to be liked. Did I have what it would take to befriend May? I wasn't sure, but I wanted to find out.

Later that morning, I told Jaime that I had made the tentative decision to talk to May.

"You're crazy," she said. "Do you know what she could do?"

"Maybe not," I replied. I didn't quite believe my own words, but I realized that, for the first time, my curiosity outweighed my fear.

After lunch, I approached May at the pencil sharpener and went for broke: I invited her to come to my house after school. "We could walk home together, if you'd like. Maybe watch the Nickelodeon Channel?" I offered. (I'd be lying if I didn't admit that I was somewhat pacified by the idea that I'd be on home turf, under the watchful eye of my parents, where little could go wrong.) Still, I was proud that I had extended the invitation.

Then, something unprecedented happened. Something that I would not have believed had I not seen it with my own eyes. May smiled. And then she said yes.

I don't remember what we watched on television, or what my mother prepared for our after-school snack. But I do know that I went from ruing the day I wore a French braid to school to realizing that it had become the catalyst for a new friendship.

May Jordan never bullied me again, and, in fact, we became pretty good friends. After spending countless afternoons at my house, I quickly realized that, yes, underneath the tall girl's armor was an insecure fifth grader who wanted nothing more than to be accepted.

I've since learned that the old adage, you can't judge a book by its cover, certainly rings true, and that someone who looks different on the outside can really be just like you.

— Courtney Conover —
Chicken Soup for the Soul: Just for Preteens

True to Myself

Our wounds are often the openings into
the best and most beautiful part of us.
–David Richo

When I was six years old, I developed a type of cancer called leukemia. It made me very ill and I spent most of my days at the Chicago Children's Hospital.

After I had two years of treatment, the cancer went into remission for almost five years. I was no longer showing signs or symptoms of the disease. But just when I thought my future looked good, my cancer came back. I had just turned eleven years old and was starting middle school. This time it hit me even harder and I had to fight to survive.

School was the last thing on my mind but I still had to complete my course work one way or another. Most of my schoolwork was done at home but when I was feeling up to it, I went to school. I couldn't walk very well, so I had to use crutches. The medicine I had to take made me weak.

I also wore a baseball hat to school because the medicine

I took made all of my hair fall out. Losing hair was not fun, especially being a girl. I was teased and even told I was in the wrong bathroom by someone who thought I looked like a boy.

The teachers and other staff members did their very best to try and help students understand my cancer. But some of the kids still chose to tease or pick on me. Dealing with cancer and school was very difficult.

Middle school was even harder to deal with because in middle school you have to switch classrooms for every subject. Since I couldn't walk well, my teachers let me leave class a few minutes before the bell rang. This gave me enough time to get to and from my next class without all the other kids rushing through the hallways.

On one particular day when I felt super weak and too tired to make it to my next class, I rested for a minute up against a wall while leaning on my crutches. Suddenly the bell rang, the classroom doors swung open, and the hallways filled up with students trying to get to their next class.

I took a deep breath and started to crutch my way through the crowd. I didn't make it very far. I remember my hat being lifted off my head and a boy shouting, "Go get it," while other kids giggled. Another kid kicked my crutch from behind me and I lost my balance. I tumbled forward and fell flat on my face. My backpack landed on top of me still strapped to my back. I lay there trying to find enough energy to get up.

The final bell rang and the doors closed. All of the students had vanished into their classrooms except for me. Still lying on the floor, I felt humiliated, in pain, and most of all, defeated.

At that very moment I hated everything about what was happening to me — my health, my weakness, my existence. I never wanted to go back to school again.

Before my cancer I thought kids' jobs were to play, have fun, and be silly. Little did I know there was more responsibility to being a child and that sometimes life wouldn't work out the way I wanted.

> I never wanted to go back to school again.

The next morning I had to make a choice. I could stay home and feel sorry for myself or I could go to school and accomplish what I had set out to do. All night long I kept thinking that if I went to school it would be just another day of humiliation, not to mention a lot of stress.

I closed my eyes and thought a while. I thought about the children I had met at the hospital who were also sick. I even thought about the kids I went to school with who had other types of problems. Unlike some of their illnesses or disabilities, mine were not permanent. I had a chance of recovering.

Right then and there I opened my eyes, sat up, and decided tomorrow was a new day and no matter how the day played out, I was going to make it, crutches and all — one step at a time.

That night I picked out my favorite T-shirt to wear, grabbed my lucky ball cap and gave myself a pep talk. I was not going to let the bullying behavior of others take me down. I told myself that my looks were just temporary, that my hair would grow back, and that one day I was going to walk again just like I used to.

To my surprise, the next school day went smoother than usual. I had regained a little bit of confidence, enough to keep trying my best and to not let others' behaviors or words bother me. I even made a new friend that month. Her name was Kristen like mine.

Eventually I got healthier and my cancer went away. Later, I became the fastest runner in my class! I even played flag football with the boys.

Tomorrow was a new day.

I didn't choose my cancer or disabilities, but I conquered them. The only thing I regretted was not telling someone about the bullying behavior. But I stayed true to myself and that is what matters.

— Kristen N. Velasquez —
Chicken Soup for the Soul: Think Positive for Kids

Chicken Soup
for the
Soul

The Normal Girl in a Not-So-Normal Chair

The hardest struggle of all is to be
something different from
what the average man is.
~Charles M. Schwab

As a twelve-and-a-half-year-old American girl, I like doing girly things. But many people aren't aware of that because they only see a twelve-and-a-half-year-old disabled girl who sits in a wheelchair. When I was in second grade, I was a speaker at an after-school program for children my age. In the beginning, the children were curious about my tubing and alarms. By the end of the program, when it was time for questions, they didn't know what to say to me. I guess they felt embarrassed. Instead of trying to talk to me, they ended up walking away and ignoring me. Unfortunately, this is a typical occurrence. Often, people would rather act like I am not there.

I use a wheelchair that has tubing to control my breathing and alarms to signal for assistance. To explain why I use this chair, with all of these devices, I need to explain my diagnosis. Before I was born, I had a stroke that affected my brain stem. It's as if my brain is a

People would rather act like I am not there.

computer, and the circuit board shorted out. My muscles don't always do what I want them to, and most definitely not in a timely manner. I can breathe but not enough to stay alive, so I use a ventilator. I can stand, but I cannot control my muscles so I would wobble around or fall over. With a ventilator I am unable to use my voice to speak, so instead I blink yes or no with my eyes. To say yes, I blink twice, and once to say no. My mom also helps me by holding my hand while I type, which takes a very long time. My alarms notify my moms that my devices are having a problem. There are different sounds for different alarms, and sometimes they can be noisy. Now you understand what it is like to be in my chair.

As a preteen girl, I enjoy putting on make-up, dressing trendy, reading about anything I can, and being outside in nature. I need a ventilator to breathe and a wheelchair to move, but I have the same interests as any other preteen girl. People seem to forget this when they see me.

Often, when I go into a store with my family, people will stare and then avert their eyes. They don't think that I see them, but they are wrong. I am aware of a lot more than they think.

People are afraid to be out of their comfort zone. They feel threatened by someone like me because they don't know what to say or do. What they don't realize is that not saying anything at all is more hurtful than anything they could have said. I want people to know that handicapped people have feelings too. If you walked into a place and everyone walked away from you, would it hurt your feelings? Well, that is how it feels for me.

> They feel threatened by someone like me because they don't know what to say or do.

By saying a simple "Hello" or asking my name, a stranger can brighten my day. This simple gesture makes me feel welcomed. I want people to know that being a preteen is hard enough, but sad stares from strangers makes it even harder. Don't feel sorry for me — my life is great! The next time you see a person in a wheelchair remember that a simple hello can go a long way. After all, a wheelchair doesn't make a person — what's in the chair is what's important.

— Dani P. d'Spirit —
Chicken Soup for the Soul: Just for Preteens

The Smile that Beat the Bully

Be excellent to each other.
~Bill and Ted's Excellent Adventure

Have you ever had a bully who scared the skin off you? The one bully who you have nightmares about? It's the face you see when you get up in the morning with your stomach all tied in knots. Rosalie Bangeter was that for me — she was a bully in every sense of the word, and I was terrified of her. She was one of the meanest girls I'd ever met, and I have a sneaking suspicion that I was not the only person in the seventh grade who lived in mortal fear of her. I'll never forget the day I saw her pulverize another student in the cafeteria. As if pounding the girl wasn't bad enough, she topped it off by dunking her head in a half-eaten tray of meatloaf and mashed potatoes.

To this day, I don't know why Rosalie hated me so much. The fact that I merely existed and had the nerve to breathe in and out seemed to tick Rosalie off, and she never missed an opportunity to threaten or ridicule me. I would hear her jeering remarks when I walked out to catch the bus home. I could feel the heat of her glare when I cowered in my seat in the cafeteria and avoided looking anywhere near her direction. I would've walked the length of two football fields to avoid coming in contact with Rosalie Bangeter if I could have, but unfortunately there just wasn't enough time to do that and still get to my fifth period class before the bell rang.

So I had to face the reality that, for two or three excruciating seconds every day, I had to walk past Rosalie Bangeter in the hall. I tried hanging out in my fourth period class a few extra seconds and walking a little slower to my locker in the hope that Rosalie would have already gone to class, but that never worked. I would still pass her. Of course, I didn't dare make eye contact with her, but I caught sight of her sneer in my peripheral vision while I scampered past. I knew it would only be a matter of time before she lashed out at me.

> I was one of those quiet, timid seventh graders.

I was one of those quiet, timid seventh graders who talked up a blue streak at home but wouldn't say two words at school. I had a couple of close friends who were just as shy as I was, and we usually huddled together and tried to stay out of everyone's way. Deep down, I was envious of those outgoing, cheerleader girls who would be the first ones to raise their hands to do a math problem on the chalkboard. I felt like life was passing me by and that if I disappeared one day, no one at school would even notice or care.

My family lived in a small town of about three thousand people, and it seemed as if my dad knew every single one of them. What was even more astonishing was that everyone seemed to know him. One day, I asked my mom how this was possible. She thought about this a minute and then said, "Well, Jenn, your dad never lets anyone stay a stranger. He talks to everyone he sees, and then he gives them that big smile of his. I guess it's contagious because people just love him."

I wanted to be more like my dad. I wanted to get to know people and to somehow leave my mark on the world. But more than anything, I was tired of being that girl who cowered in a corner and got picked on.

I thought about what my mom had said. I knew I had to take action, but how? There was no way I could just go to school one day and start talking to everybody. Forget for a moment that they would have thought I was a raving lunatic — I knew that, as good as my intentions were, I would never be able to force the words out of my mouth. So, I caught hold of the phrase where she talked about his smile. I could smile. I mean, everyone could do that, right? I decided to try it out, but I knew that there was only one way to go to the heart of my fears. I would take my experiment straight to the biggest bully of all — Rosalie Bangeter.

I don't think I heard a single word my math teacher said that day in fourth period because I was too busy thinking about what I was about to do. Finally, the bell rang. I gathered my books and headed to my locker. My heart was pounding in my chest, and my hands were so sweaty I was afraid I'd drop my books. Somehow, I managed to shove my math book in the locker and pull out my English book. I ran my tongue over my teeth that felt dryer than the Mojave Desert. Then I did a practice smile that I was sure looked more like a grimace. I took a deep breath and willed my feet to keep moving forward.

I saw her in the distance coming toward me, looking as mean as ever. For the first time in my life, I made eye contact with her, and then I did it! I actually managed to squeak out a smile through my chattering teeth. Rosalie looked downright shocked, and then she scowled. I hurried past, sure that she was going to turn around and pounce on me. I don't think I took another breath until I made it to my next class and collapsed in the chair.

> I actually managed to squeak out a smile through my chattering teeth.

The next day, I tried again. This time, my teeth weren't chattering quite so badly. Rosalie was no longer surprised, but her snarl remained. This went on for several days, until one day, she didn't glower. I hurried past her. Maybe she was in too big of a hurry today, I thought.

The next day, she didn't glower at me either. In fact, she gave me a little half-smile for my effort. Over the next few weeks, Rosalie actually started smiling back. And then came that memorable day when I got the nerve to nod and say hi. I couldn't believe it! She said hi back! At the end of the year, Rosalie looked me up and asked me to sign her yearbook.

In the years that followed, I broke out of my shell one small chip at a time. I made many new friends and became an active participant in my classes. Looking back now, I can trace it all to that fateful day when I had the courage to smile in the face of the bully. The next time you're in a jam, give it a try — it's amazing how far a smile can go.

— Jennifer Youngblood —
Chicken Soup for the Soul: Teens Talk Middle School

A smile is like
a boomerang.
When you throw
one out there,
it almost always
comes back.

~Amy Newmark

The Nice Popular Girl

It's nice to be important, but it's more
important to be nice.
-Author Unknown

My closest friend when I was little was Priscilla. She and I were friends through all of elementary school.

Priscilla was always the most popular girl in our grade, not just our class, but in our whole grade. I remember one time when I bought a new pair of shoes, which she liked, and she went out and bought the same ones. Mine were black, but she said they were out of black in her size so she bought them in navy blue. All the other girls in our class saw her shoes and copied them, and within the next couple of weeks most of

All the other girls in our class saw her shoes and copied them.

the girls in our sixth grade class were wearing those shoes, in navy blue. I was the only one with black ones. I remember thinking how bizarre it was that everyone copied her shoes, right down to the color.

I remember watching Priscilla in the lunch line too. We had a lot of choices in the cafeteria, and no one knew what was cool. Were we too cool to drink milk? Which were the right foods to choose? We were all so insecure. Priscilla just did what she wanted to do. One day I was in the line behind her and another girl who was trying to become Priscilla's best friend, replacing me, or at least I thought so. That girl didn't have milk on her tray but then she saw Priscilla take milk, so she put her juice back and took milk instead. Then Priscilla changed her mind and put the milk back. So the other girl put her milk back too. I was disgusted by this and thought it was ridiculous to copy someone to that extent.

Priscilla was popular with the boys too. We all had crushes on the same boys but they always ended up with Priscilla. Since we were young, that just meant that they officially "liked" her and talked to her at school. This was before texting, and boys didn't call girls on the phone at that age, as that would have been terrifying. But in school, these boys were officially with Priscilla. And she seemed completely comfortable talking to them, not nervous at all. When I "went steady" with a boy in seventh grade I was so embarrassed I could barely speak to him.

I know that the "popular" girls are often the mean ones too, but this was not the case with Priscilla. She was nice to everyone. There was a small group of semi-popular and very mean girls, but they were separate from Priscilla and me and our closest friends.

It was only decades later, when I found Priscilla 2,000 miles away by searching for her on the Internet, that I learned something shocking to me. Priscilla had no idea she was popular.

> Priscilla had no idea she was popular.

She didn't know that the other girls copied her; she didn't know that her "boyfriends" were the boys that all the girls were crushing on. She was clueless, and it turns out she had been very insecure during those years. She was even afraid to talk to those cute boys.

It was a real eye opener for me. The most popular girl in the grade was insecure, completely unaware of her influence and status among us.

It just goes to show, you never know what's going on inside someone else's head, even if it seems obvious.

— Amy Newmark —
Chicken Soup for the Soul: Think Positive for Kids

MEET OUR CONTRIBUTORS

We are pleased to introduce you to the writers whose stories were compiled from our past books to create this new collection. These bios were the ones that ran when the stories were originally published. They were current as of the publication dates of those books.

Brianna Abbott is a normal teenager who likes to laugh and run in the rain. She loves her family and her friends with all her heart and plans to continue writing for the rest of her life.

Julia K. Agresto is a Communications and Marketing Specialist for a renowned medical center in Massachusetts, as well as a freelance writer/journalist. She graduated from the University of New Hampshire in 2009 with a degree in English/ Journalism and Sociology.

Ms. **Jackson Beard** is an eighth grader. Jackson is an avid reader who also enjoys long distance running, African dance, and cooking. She is also passionate about global politics and environmental issues.

Lisa Bell received her B.S. in Business Management, with honors, from the University of Phoenix in 2005. She is a freelance writer and lives in Texas. Lisa enjoys anything outdoors, volunteers with local organizations and writes both fiction and nonfiction. Learn more at www.bylisabell.com or e-mail her at LisaBell@bylisabell.com.

Valerie D. Benko is a freelance writer from western Pennsylvania. Her stories have appeared in four *Chicken Soup for the Soul* anthologies as well as *Patchwork Path* editions including *Christmas Stocking*, *Treasure Box* and the soon to be released *Mother's Life*. Learn more at valeriebenko.weebly.com.

Caitlin Brown, a sixteen-year-old homeschooled student, enjoys reading, playing paintball, baking, producing movies featuring her three younger siblings and writing children's stories and novels. She works yearlong with www.OperationChristmasChild.org filling shoeboxes with gifts for needy children overseas. E-mail Caitlin at shoeboxgirl@comcast.net.

Leigh Ann Bryant is a wife and mother of three sons. She received her BSN from the University of Texas at Arlington. She loves the Lord and is very active with the youth at her church. She loves to write, travel, and watch her sons do gymnastics. E-mail her at bryant_leighann@msn.com.

Andrea Canale is currently in her last year of college, studying Cultural Anthropology. She hopes to continue her hobby of helping others by joining the Peace Corps. Andrea enjoys drumming, reading, and cooking. She was first published in three *Chicken Soup for the Soul* books in 2008.

Zulema Anahy Carlos is a high school senior. She is

an outgoing and outspoken girl who enjoys helping people, working with children, dancing and singing. Zulema also enjoys writing nonfiction because she's able to express her feelings, thoughts and talk about the real world.

Beth Cato is an active member of the Science Fiction & Fantasy Writers of America, and a frequent contributor to the *Chicken Soup for the Soul* series. She's originally from Hanford, CA, but now resides in Buckeye, AZ with her husband and son. Connect with her through www.bethcato.com.

Courtney Conover is a freelance writer and yoga practitioner who resides in Michigan with her husband, Scott. The couple eagerly awaits the birth of their first child this fall. This is Courtney's fourth contribution to the *Chicken Soup for the Soul* series. Learn more at www.courtneyconover.com.

D'ette Corona is the Associate Publisher of Chicken Soup for the Soul. She received her Bachelor of Science degree in business management. D'ette has been happily married for twenty-one years and has a sixteen-year-old son whom she adores.

Maddy Curtis dreams of becoming a professional singer by attending Catholic University of America for her Bachelor of Music degree in Vocal Performance. She is the ninth child in her huge family of twelve and hopes to become an opera singer and use her talents to benefit children with special needs. E-mail her at maddycurtis93@gmail.com.

Dani d'Spirit lives with her moms, brother and two sisters in rural southern Delaware. She loves reading, outdoors, cultures, history, science and world peace. Right now she is looking at a career as a cultural liaison for the U.S. State Department. E-mail her at daniwoodsprite@earthlink.net.

Suzanne De Vita received her B.A. degree in communications from Quinnipiac University. A lifelong writer with a passion for working with children, she plans to pursue a career in public relations with an emphasis on youth programming. E-mail her at suzdev27@gmail.com.

Born in Los Angeles in 1993, **Jack Ettlinger** now lives in Toronto. A total sports enthusiast, Jack's passion is hockey and he recently scored the winning goal to capture first place in his high school city championships. In 2012, Jack sang his way to the semi-final round on *Canada's Got Talent*.

Victoria Fedden received her MFA degree in Creative Writing from Florida Atlantic University in 2009. She lives in Fort Lauderdale, FL. She has had several stories published in the *Chicken Soup for the Soul* series as well as many other publications, and is the author of *Amateur Night at the Bubblegum Kittikat*, a memoir for adults.

Marcela Dario Fuentes was adopted from Honduras. She is a professional musician and performance resident in bassoon at Carnegie Mellon University, and her stories have appeared in several previous *Chicken Soup for the Soul* books. She enjoys hearing from her readers at wereallwright@gmail.com.

Jody Fuller was born and raised in Opelika, AL. He is a comedian, speaker, writer, and soldier with three tours of duty in Iraq. He currently holds the rank of Captain in the Alabama National Guard. Jody is also a lifetime stutterer. E-mail him at jody@jodyfuller.com.

Carmella de los Angeles Guiol is a Floridian gardener, dancer, adventurer, photographer, and writer. She has traveled to five continents and has worked as an artisan baker, organic farmer, and yacht deck hand. You can often find her kayaking the Hillsborough River, but you can always find her at therestlesswriter.com.

Freelance writer and piano teacher **Wendy Hobday Haugh** can't wait to share these stories with her grandchildren: Marissa, Charlie, Lilli and Max. She hopes this book will help kids everywhere by offering them encouragement, fresh insights, and smiles galore. E-mail her at whhaugh@nycap.rr.com.

Valerie Howlett graduated from Hampshire College last year after studying creative writing, children's literature, and children's theater. She worked for a theater company and a law office before finding her wonderful position at Chicken Soup for the Soul! She loves showtunes, chilling with her younger siblings, curling up with a good book and, of course, writing.

Jackson Jarvis is fourteen years old, into surfing and classic rock (he thinks he should've been born in the 1960s). An aspiring music producer, he's also written three yet-to-be published books including *The Book of Bad Ideas* and *The Weird Stuff I Do*. He lives in New York State with his mom, Joelle, and his dad Eric is his guardian angel.

Cassie Jones graduated from Texas A&M University in 2014 and now teaches in Houston, TX. She enjoys writing, reading, and playing video games in her spare time.

Stacie Joslin grew up in Wasco, CA, with a love for reading and writing. She is an administrative assistant in her hometown.

Stacie is married with four children and she enjoys traveling, writing and spending time with her family. Stacie is currently working on writing novels. E-mail her at stacielopez@att.net.

Rachel Joyce attended middle school in Colorado. She loves to write and follow politics with her family. Rachel plans to combine these two passions and become a political journalist. She lives with her mother, father, sister and dog Ginger.

MJ Keenan is a retired elementary school teacher, having taught kindergarten through third grade for many years. MJ enjoys writing, reading, walking, and spending time with her husband Ken and their children, grandchildren, and four dogs.

Mary Elizabeth Laufer has a degree in English Education from SUNY Albany. When she's not writing, she works as a substitute teacher for the Osceola County school district in Florida. Her stories and poems have appeared in magazines, newspapers and several anthologies.

B.J. Lee lives in Florida with her poet husband, Malcolm Deeley, and poodles, JoJo and Clementine. She has fifty poems published in magazines such as *Highlights for Children*; and anthologies such as *And the Crowd Goes Wild!* and *The Rhysling Anthology*. You can read more of her poems at www.childrensauthorbjlee.com.

Austin Nicholas Lees is an active fourth grader. He enjoys soccer, street hockey, snowboarding, and volunteering. He is active in his church and loves Jesus. He lives with his mom, dad, and two dogs, Cooper and Winston.

Kathy Linker received her B.A. in Psychology from The University of Western Ontario, a graduate degree in Clinical

Art Therapy and her Master in Education from the University of Victoria. She has traveled the globe extensively and is writing inspirational stories about her adventures. E-mail her at kathylinker@hotmail.com.

Barbara LoMonaco has worked for Chicken Soup for the Soul as an editor since 1998. She has co-authored two *Chicken Soup for the Soul* book titles and has had stories published in numerous other titles. Barbara is a graduate of the University of Southern California and has a teaching credential.

Elizabeth M. is twelve years old. She currently attends middle school in the 7th grade. Elizabeth loves reading *Chicken Soup for the Soul* books and is very athletic and has played soccer since she was five but recently found a new interest in basketball.

Scott Neumyer is a freelance journalist whose work has appeared in print and online publications like *Parenting* magazine, *New Jersey Family*, *ESPN*, *Esquire*, *Wired*, *Details*, *Babble*, and many more. He lives in central New Jersey with his wife and daughter. He also loves bacon far too much. E-mail him at scott@scottneumyer.com.

Sylvia Ney received her B.S. in Mass Communication from Lamar University in 2000. She lives in Texas with her husband and two children. She enjoys reading, writing, traveling and spending time with family and friends. She writes in a variety of genres. You can visit her blog at http://writinginwonderland.blogspot.com.

Shirley Oakes is a wife, mother, grandmother and great-grandmother who enjoys her family. She and her daughter are co-owners of the Family Affair Day Care/Pre-School. She enjoys doing family history work, sewing, painting and gardening. She has also written a children's book.

Denise Reich is an amateur trapeze artist, compulsive traveler and rock music fan. She'd like to learn to surf this year. Denise has written for many publications in the USA and elsewhere, including several *Chicken Soup for the Soul* titles, the anthology *She's Shameless*, *Bunker Hill*, and *Pology*.

Chloe Rosenberg lives in Connecticut with her wonderful parents, two brothers, three cats and two dogs. When she is not traveling, she is usually reading, cooking or chasing her brothers for dunking her kitten in the toilet. She hopes to become either a travel guidebook writer, lawyer or acclaimed pastry chef.

Bill Rouhana is the CEO of Chicken Soup for the Soul and is grateful to his parents for giving him the bike in his story, teaching him important lessons about living and for many other things.

Lindy Schneider loves throwing big parties with extensive invitation lists! She is an award-winning freelance writer and illustrator with her work appearing in books and magazines and even on Red Vines candy packages! E-mail her at lindy_schn@yahoo.com or learn more at www.lindysbooks.com.

Tracie Skarbo's stories have appeared in several of the *Chicken Soup for the Soul* books in the past, her book *Harmonious Flight* was released in 2011 and a second titled *Pulp Tattoos* will be released later this year. She lives on Vancouver Island with her family and enjoys running, climbing and photography.

Kristen N. Velasquez is a teacher, poet, and writer. Her story, "Backseat Driver," was published in *Chicken Soup for the Soul: Angels Among Us*. Kristen is a cancer survivor and advocates for childhood cancer patients and children with special needs. View her current projects at www.operation-gold.com and redfeathermarket.com.

Jude Walsh writes memoir, personal essay, and self-help. Her writing is published in numerous literary magazines and anthologies, including *The Magic of Memoir* (2016) and *Chicken Soup for the Soul: Inspiration for Teachers* (2017). She lives in Dayton, OH with her son and three lively dogs. Learn more at www.judewalsh-writer.com.

Dallas Woodburn is a writer, editor, teacher and literacy advocate living in the San Francisco Bay Area. To date, she has been a proud contributor to more than two dozen titles in the *Chicken Soup for the Soul* series. She regularly blogs about simple, joyful, healthy living at DaybyDayMasterpiece.com.

Jennifer Youngblood is the co-author of *Livin' in High Cotton* and of the bestselling novel, Stoney Creek, Alabama. She and her mom, Sandra Poole, write together. They're currently working on their third and fourth novels. A native of Alabama, Jennifer currently lives in Hawaii with her husband and children.

MEET
AMY NEWMARK

Amy Newmark is the bestselling author, editor-in-chief, and publisher of the *Chicken Soup for the Soul* book series. Since 2008, she has published 165 new books, most of them national bestsellers in the U.S. and Canada, more than doubling the number of Chicken Soup for the Soul titles in print today. She is also the author of *Simply Happy*, a crash course in Chicken Soup for the Soul advice and wisdom that is filled with easy-to-implement, practical tips for enjoying a better life.

Amy is credited with revitalizing the Chicken Soup for the Soul brand, which has been a publishing industry phenomenon since the first book came out in 1993. By compiling inspirational and aspirational true stories curated from ordinary people who have had extraordinary experiences, Amy has kept the twenty-seven-year-old Chicken Soup for the Soul brand fresh and relevant.

Amy graduated *magna cum laude* from Harvard University where she majored in Portuguese and minored in French. She then embarked on a three-decade career as a Wall Street analyst, a hedge fund manager, and a corporate executive in the technology field. She is a Chartered Financial Analyst.

Her return to literary pursuits was inevitable, as her honors thesis in college involved traveling throughout Brazil's impoverished northeast region, collecting stories from regular people. She is delighted to have come full circle in her writing career — from collecting stories "from the people" in Brazil as a twenty-year-old to, three decades later, collecting stories "from the people" for Chicken Soup for the Soul.

When Amy and her husband Bill, the CEO of Chicken Soup for the Soul, are not working, they are visiting their four grown children and their grandchildren.

Follow Amy on Twitter @amynewmark. Listen to her free podcast — "Chicken Soup for the Soul with Amy Newmark" — on Apple Podcasts, Google Play, the Podcasts app on iPhone, or by using your favorite podcast app on other devices.

SHARING HAPPINESS, INSPIRATION, AND HOPE

Real people sharing real stories, every day, all over the world. In 2007, *USA Today* named *Chicken Soup for the Soul* one of the five most memorable books in the last quarter-century. With over 100 million books sold to date in the U.S. and Canada alone, more than 250 titles in print, and translations into nearly fifty languages, "chicken soup for the soul®" is one of the world's best-known phrases.

Today, twenty-seven years after we first began sharing happiness, inspiration and hope through our books, we continue to delight our readers with new titles, but have also evolved beyond the bookshelves with super premium pet food, television shows, a podcast, video journalism from aplus.com, licensed products, and free movies and TV shows on our Popcornflix and Crackle apps. We are busy "changing the world one story at a time®." Thanks for reading!

SHARE WITH US

We all have had Chicken Soup for the Soul moments in our lives. If you would like to share your story or poem with millions of people around the world, go to chickensoup.com and click on Submit Your Story. You may be able to help another reader and become a published author at the same time. Some of our past contributors have launched writing and speaking careers from the publication of their stories in our books!

We only accept story submissions via our website. They are no longer accepted via mail or fax. Visit our website, www.chickensoup.com, and click on Submit Your Story for our writing guidelines and a list of topics we are working on.

To contact us regarding other matters, please send us an e-mail through webmaster@chickensoupforthesoul.com, or fax or write us at:

Chicken Soup for the Soul
P.O. Box 700
Cos Cob, CT 06807-0700
Fax: 203-861-7194

One more note from your friends at Chicken Soup for the Soul: Occasionally, we receive an unsolicited book manuscript from one of our readers, and we would like to respectfully inform you that we do not accept unsolicited manuscripts, and we must discard the ones that appear.

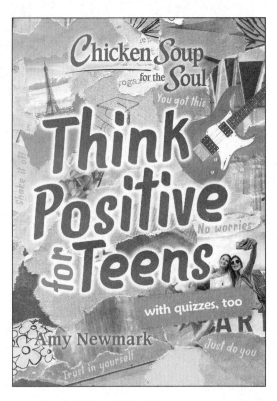

Paperback: 978-1-61159-996-1

eBook: 978-1-61159-296-2

More positive thinking

Paperback: 978-1-61159-927-5
eBook: 978-1-61159-229-0

for preteens and parents

Chicken Soup for the Soul

Teens Talk
MIDDLE SCHOOL

101 Stories of Life, Love,
and Learning for Younger Teens

Jack Canfield,
Mark Victor Hansen,
Madeline Clapps & Valerie Howlett

Paperback: 978-1-935096-26-9
eBook: 978-1-61159-155-2

about kids your age

Chicken Soup for the Soul

Changing the world one story at a time®
www.chickensoup.com